The
ANGer
Box

Sensory turmoil and pain in autism

Phoebe Caldwell

The ANGER Box

Sensory turmoil and pain in autism

© Phoebe Caldwell

Published by:
Pavilion Publishing and Media Ltd
Rayford House
School Road
Hove
East Sussex
BN3 5HX
Tel: 01273 434943
Fax: 01273 227308
Email: info@pavpub.com

Published 2014 and 2015.

A catalogue record for this book is available from the British Library.

ISBN: 978-1-909810-44-0

Pavilion is the leading training and development provider and publisher in the health, social care and allied fields, providing a range of innovative training solutions underpinned by sound research and professional values. We aim to put our customers first, through excellent customer service and value.

Author: Phoebe Caldwell
Editor: Mike Benge, Pavilion Publishing and Media Ltd
Cover design: Emma Dawe, Pavilion Publishing and Media Ltd
Page layout and typesetting: Phil Morash, Pavilion Publishing and Media Ltd
Printing: CMP Digital Print Solutions

Cover image courtesy of William Grainger, age 6.

'It's not so much what we learn but what we do with what we learn'.

Donna Williams

Contents

Foreword

By Dr Elspeth Bradley

During the past three decades, Dr Phoebe Caldwell has been providing interventions and support to people with autism and learning disabilities (LD) experiencing distress in their lives.

These individuals are invariably described as challenging services or as having challenging or problem behaviours. Phoebe takes an alternative view, noting that 'most of the individuals I am asked to see are on the autistic spectrum, many of whom are extremely distressed and, seeing the world round them as hostile, sometimes respond to it with outbreaks of violent behaviours'. Phoebe thus resonates with a perspective that essentially places the experience of the individual central to our understanding of why they are doing what they are doing, rather than making interpretations of their behaviour based on our biased non-autism/LD viewpoint.

As part of understanding the experience of people with autism and LD, Phoebe has absorbed herself in biographical narratives of self-advocates with autism (eg. Donna Williams, Temple Grandin and many others). With this appreciation, combined with the courage and willingness to reflect deeply into her own sensory experience, emotional responses, behaviours and thoughts (a pursuit which today would be considered mindfulness practice), Phoebe has been able, using an Intensive Interaction approach, to engage with individuals with autism and LD in distress. Often for the first time, such individuals experience a sense of real belonging in the social world and the behaviours which others have found so difficult fade away. Families and care providers feel empowered to continue this engagement enriching the lives of individuals they support as well as their own. As Phoebe notes in her work with Gabriel, a young man who stopped violently and repeatedly hitting his head against hard surfaces: 'Real equality is when you are using the same emotional language as each other and you value each other'.

During these same decades I have also been working with people with autism and LD but as a clinical academic LD psychiatrist. I have also been asked to see people referred because of problem or challenging behaviours, the latter description very much reflecting the outside-in perspective of medical practice and the community at large. I first came across one of Phoebe's books at a conference in London and it immediately caught my attention. Not only was it addressing an issue about which I and my colleagues in LD psychiatry were very familiar – and equally familiar with the feelings of inadequacy in providing some effective intervention – but it was also outlining a very different approach. I was intrigued, but the language and content felt somewhat uncomfortable. For example, the author was describing in simple terms what I had come to appreciate as complex biological phenomena, and she was bold in making connections where I felt more caution was needed. In essence, the author was inviting the reader to engage with an experience outside of their own – in particular with that of individuals with autism and LD – and to recognise the challenge in trying to articulate and share our human experience when there are no words. In later years when I would question Phoebe about this she would typically say, 'Try it out for yourself!' In other words, engage in the behaviour and experience the associated sensations, perceptions and feelings.

While we may recognise that feeling connected to others also occurs in the absence of spoken language – as is evidenced by the mother and the baby engaged in an intimate moment through reciprocal babble, facial communication and other body language – somehow we fail to recognise the existence of an emotional life in people who struggle to communicate whether because of autism or LD. And this is at great cost to them and to those who support them, as emotional regulation embedded in meaningful relationships provides the context within which curiosity, motivation and learning are nurtured and nourished. In the absence of such recognition and validation, distress and problem behaviours arise.

While Phoebe's previous books have focused on interventions in response to particular presentations and symptoms, *The Anger Box* leaps forward, and provides a fascinating and stimulating creative synthesis of emerging neurobiological understanding applied to recurring themes such as sensory sensitivities and distortions, self-injury and pain, that have emerged in her work over the years. In this book we are again reminded of the wealth and depth of Phoebe's experience working with people with autism and LD, as well as her intimate knowledge of the narratives of people with autism. When observing Phoebe at work she is totally present for the individual she is working with and absorbed in their experience while trying to work out what intervention, from their perspective, might be helpful. Her method might be considered practice-based evidence as she tirelessly and gently tests out hypotheses when engaging with her atypically communicating partner. Her understanding from this absorption is detailed and nuanced and perhaps it is no wonder that she is then able to make what might appear to be stunning leaps, or 'eureka moments', as to possible neurobiological underpinnings of the phenomena she is observing clinically. I once asked her how she came to bring certain observations and ideas together and she commented it was not so much bringing things together as things falling into place – like pieces in a jigsaw. I once observed such a eureka moment when Phoebe had occasion to review a poster map (used in medical teaching) of the nerve innervation of different parts of the human body. This followed closely a visit to see a child who would scream for hours and slap her head and face very hard, causing injury. On seeing the poster Phoebe immediately recognised that the pattern of the child's behaviour (and some others she had seen in the past) matched the pattern of specific nerve innervation of the face and neck. Phoebe, mindful also of the reports by self-advocates with autism describing painful discomfort around the neck and face area which increased when stressed and feeling overwhelmed, started to reflect on whether the trigeminal nerve may be implicated. Subsequent exploration of the families of some of these individuals revealed a tantalising prevalence of trigeminal neuralgia. This intriguing series of observations coming together like pieces of the puzzle is one of many shared in *The Anger Box* and invites our further attention and research.

This book will, I think, excite and inspire and be helpful to a broad range of readers including those with autism and their families and other care providers providing support, members of the multidisciplinary teams supporting individuals in distress, and those interested in behavioural neurobiology or researching the mind and the brain, especially as this applies to autism and LD.

While others might be contemplating retirement, Phoebe says she keeps working 'because it is possible to bring calm into their lives and to teach others to do so'.

The Anger Box is a welcome addition to understanding the distress experienced by people with autism and LD and in helping all of us bring calm into their lives.

Dr Elspeth Bradley PhD, FRCPC, FRCPsych
Psychiatrist-in-Chief, Surrey Place Centre
Associate Professor, Department of Psychiatry
University of Toronto, Canada
e.bradley@utoronto.ca

Who is this book for?

There has recently been a shift away from considering autism from the point of view of its presentation and symptoms, towards an increasing exploration and understanding of sensory issues underpinning the condition and its physiological and neurobiological roots[1]. The central theme of this book differs from previous ones I have written on autism in that its focus is on the one hand the experience of physical pain and emotional distress and trauma consequent to developmental deficits and sensory distortions – and on the other, the responses of society to resulting behavioural outcomes. What I have tried to do is to marry theory and practice, placing new ways of looking at the autistic spectrum alongside extensive experience of engaging with children and adults on the spectrum.

The Anger Box is a book of ideas spanning a wide field of research. Some of it is speculative. I hope it will be interesting for professionals who, because of the volume of research pouring out of their journals, can get corralled inside their own disciplines – but I have tried to write it in such a way that it will be readable to parents and those who have a general interest in autism. I hope that it will also be of interest to some of my autistic friends. When we add new pieces to a jigsaw, we begin to make out new patterns.

I have followed the custom of altering names, except where individuals and families have decided to use their own, on the grounds that their contribution is important and they or their parents do not wish to conceal their identity, a choice with which I sympathise. I value their contributions and I am pleased to attribute them to those to whom they belong. Where relevant, I have revisited some interventions previously published – but much of the practice described is new. However, books like this are not just the work of their author. We build on each other's work. So I want to pay tribute to all the people who have generously talked to me about their

---

1   Caminha RC & Lampreia C (2012) Findings on sensory deficits in autism: implications for understanding the disorder. *Psychology and Neuroscience* **5** (2) 31–237.

autism, as well as those who have given me so many ideas and so much help. Particularly it is for William, for his ideas and drawings of the Anger Box and Good Box – and for Chris and Amy – and for Elspeth Bradley, Nicole Whitman, Jemma Swales, Janet Gurney, Michelle O'Neill, Damian Milton, Philippine Sowerby and many, many others who have fed me with information and laid the foundations for my thoughts.

Thank you also to Holly for technical help. Finally, the development of this practice could not have happened without 30 or so years of continuing support in a variety of ways from the Norah Fry Research Institute, Bristol University.

Chapter one: The Anger Box

William

William is drawing his anger box, the shape of a cornflakes packet. In place of the iconic cockerel, a face snarls from the front, squinting with rage. As he draws, he explains in quite a detached way how it lives in his chest, and that when he is getting upset the top opens and the anger flows out, up into his head and down his arms, into his elbows and on down into his wrists and knuckles and his fingertips. (A clever child, William is six and these are the actual words he uses to describe his body parts.)

He says that once the box is open, he can't stop it. His hand stiffens as he demonstrates the progress of the pain, wiping one arm with the other hand, almost in horror, as if he was trying to obliterate it.

William's description of the actual sensations involved when he loses control are in fact very similar to those described by both Donna Williams[2] and Gunilla Gerland[3], although they locate the starting point in the nape of the neck. In particular, all three describe sensations that radiate out from a central point into the arms and elbows and so on down. Donna describes how they, 'spread to every fibre of my body like cracks in an earthquake', with the sensations spreading down to her feet. 'My eyes frantically look for meaning, my head seems to explode.'

The purpose of this book, *The Anger Box*, is to ask a number of questions about autism. I do not have all the answers, but I hope that it will lead us to reflect on the autistic spectrum in ways that are helpful. I make no apology for the fact that it will have to cover some familiar ground in order to reach a little further into the paradoxes and discontinuities that are part of the

---

2   Williams D (1994) *Somebody Somewhere*. Toronto: Doubleday (p99). (See Appendix 1.)
3   Gerland G (1996) *A Real Person*. London: Souvenir Press (p56). (See Appendix 1.)

autistic condition. To save repeating previous books too much, readers not familiar with the 'insider's' point of view of autism will find the information they need in **Appendix 1: An inside out approach**.

Central to autism is that the brain finds it difficult to process too much incoming information and goes into sensory overload, a bottleneck where unprocessed images and sounds and sensations clog the brain systems. This situation arises not only as a result of both hyper and hypo-sensitivities to any one of the senses (including the internal sensations that arise from emotional overload) but also because the brain is unable to prioritise and filter out unnecessary stimuli. So, for example, someone on the spectrum may be hypersensitive to sounds, hearing noises like the hum of machines or electricity in the walls. Visually they may see detail rather than getting a whole picture. The exact nature of sensory sensitivity varies from individual to individual.

'My brain is like dial-up modem. If you feed it too much data it crashes.'[4]

Under pressure, the brain casts around for a coherent pattern, something that it recognises in order to prevent being tipped into what is described variously as tantrums, losing it, kicking off, meltdown, fragmentation or, more accurately, 'the autonomic storm'. First it looks for some way of reducing sensory inputs that are so distressing it by shifting its point of focus. If this fails, the brain tips into self-defence mode, which shows up in a number of different ways but are usually specific to a particular individual.

Among other aspects of the autistic condition, I want to look at what it is that determines exactly how the body tries to fend off the confusion that results from sensory overload. Why do some take refuge in repetitive behaviour and others run away? Why do some people with autism shut down completely, while others apparently 'blow their fuses'? And why do some hit themselves and others attack those close to them? What is happening inside the individual that determines how they respond to what they may perceive as life-threatening?

These are important questions if we are to escape the straightjacket of viewing autism in the light of behaviours that are the outcome of its effects rather than its causes.

---

4   WeirdGirlCyndi (2007) *Sensory Overload Simulation* [online]. Available at: www.youtube.com/watch?v=BPDTEuotHe0 (accessed January 2014).

As a practitioner, my first contact with caregivers is usually in the form of an enquiry as to how staff can cope with a particular behaviour, because behaviour is uppermost in their minds. The query, 'What do we do about John?' takes precedence over the question of why John is attacking people, self-injuring, getting stuck in awkward positions, unable to continue with a task or simply hiding.

Before addressing how we can contain him I shall be asking *why* he behaves so strangely? What is going on in his mind? Is there anything we can do to help reduce the obvious distress that he is clearly experiencing?

Alister in meltdown

Nearly a year ago, I worked with an eight-year-old boy, Alister[5]. Alister, who has ASD, is deeply distressed, lying on the floor in the school foyer, kicking out, bellowing and periodically shouting, 'No, no, no'. Four staff are standing around him but he is resisting all his teacher's patient efforts to persuade him to stand up and come to his class. I suggest they move back and, standing out of reach of his flailing limbs, I use his non-verbal language to engage his attention. Each time he bellows I answer him empathetically, but my voice is softer and lower than his. After a minute or so he quite suddenly takes off his shoe, slams it on the floor and looks at me defiantly. This is good news in a way, since up until now he has appeared to be completely disconnected. Refusing to be drawn into a custodial role of trying to put his shoe back on, I turn to his shoe and, using one of his sounds, empathise with its solitary plight.

Alister looks extremely surprised, picks up the shoe and puts it on again immediately, but in doing so, he folds in the back of it on his heel so that it is uncomfortable. Using a curved finger to make an accompanying gesture, I speak to him for the first time, saying, 'Shall I make it comfy for you?' He promptly sticks out his foot for me to do so. He then resumes his bellowing but it is more muted. I continue to answer each time. After a few more sounds, he suddenly gets up, places his hand in his teacher's, abruptly says 'sorry', and walks back to his classroom. Normally his distressed periods last for up to an hour. This whole episode was over in five minutes. (However, the tone of his apology is interesting: both his teacher and I notice independently that the word sounds detached from himself, empty, as if he is aware that this is a 'noise' appropriate to the occasion but is unaware of its affective content. He does not sound as if he feels it.)

---

5   Caldwell P (2012) *Delicious Conversations*. Brighton: Pavilion Publishing.

On the face of it, we have a child having a tantrum. However, if we start to unpick what is happening, a rather different picture emerges.

Talking to Alister's parents, they explain that they have felt that it will help him to fit in to society if he is good mannered and to this end they have laid emphasis on certain patterns of behaviour. For example, he has been encouraged to hold open the door and let others through before going through himself. He has taken this on board and it has become part of his routine.

On this particular day, Alister comes in to school at a time which would normally be quiet – but today there is an alteration in the timetable and he is met by a large number of children leaving the school at an unusual time and is swept aside. He finds himself in a severe predicament: on the one hand he has in his brain the message he has learned telling him that he must hold open the door – and on the other, the message that he cannot fulfil this requirement.

These contradictory messages place an overwhelming strain on his processing system: his brain becomes a battleground, tipping him into a painful autonomic storm that sweeps aside his ability to behave in the ways that he knows are expected of him.

Alister is now at the mercy of an unregulated sympathetic nervous maelstrom with all its attendant physical distress. Desperate to emerge, he shouts, 'no, no, no', and lashes out at anyone who comes near or speaks to him since proximity and speech only increase his sensory overload, processing difficulties and attendant physical and psychological distress. At this point I intervene and use the technique known as Intensive Interaction. Intensive Interaction bypasses speech and works instead with body language, recognising and responding not just to what the individual is doing but also to the way they are doing it – and what this tells us about their internal affective state; how they feel. Contact is made using familiar signals, ones that are part of their personal repertoire or 'vocabulary', which do not add to the difficulties the brain has in processing incoming signals. The most effective way to use it is not simply to 'copy' but to respond in a way that is based on their sound or movement or rhythm but with slight differences. Imitation will get attention but the 'alteration' will intrigue the brain sufficiently to shift attention outwards onto the source outside itself. (Musicians have a name for this – 'call and response' – where a phrase is delivered by one musician and the response from another is basically the same, but slightly altered.) The effect has been described as like being thrown a life-belt in a stormy sea.

First of all, I simply insert a contingent response to each of Alister's utterances. These capture his attention, shifting his brain's focus outward, away from his inner sensory despair. He becomes aware of something in his environment that he recognises and that his brain can latch on to. But his body is still flooded with adrenalin, and his first contact with me is angry and defiant. He is taken completely by surprise when my response – which he recognises because it is part of his own body language – continues to be one of empathy, but this time for his displaced shoe: slamming it on the floor is his way of representing to me how and possibly where he feels himself to be. He immediately replaces it. We are in contact with each other and he is no longer trapped in his inner conflict. Now I can talk to him but I use gesture to support my speech. Re-orientated, he is able to return to class.

From the point of view of practice, it is the element of surprise in this intervention that is critical in re-orientating his attention from his inner world to connecting with the world outside. By the time I insert the surprise factor (empathy with the shoe), we are sufficiently tuned in to each other for his brain to anticipate a familiar response from me to each of his utterances. At this critical point, however, what he gets from me is a response sufficiently related to avoid breaking continuity, but strange enough to jolt him out of his internal conflict. He stands up and is ready to go back to his class.

Alister is clearly a child who is extremely anxious to please his parents and to do what they ask of him. The difficulty arises when circumstances prevent his fulfilling their expectations. Speaking to Alister's parents, I suggested that he might be less anxious – and consequently less likely to become sensorily overloaded – if they eased up on insisting on his conforming to particular patterns of behaviour. A couple of months later his mother tells me that, following this advice, he is much more relaxed.

Two themes emerge from this account. The most obvious is the approach used to defuse a critical situation – Intensive Interaction.

But rather than laying the emphasis on how to cope with disturbed behaviour, the second theme, the one that is the focus of this book, recognises the need to examine instead the *context of behaviour* if we are to hope to understand it – and possibly find ways of assisting the individual out of their distress. Because what we are still calling 'challenging behaviour' in people with autism is a response to sensory overload that should more properly be thought of as 'distressed behaviour'. And distressed though it may be (and distressing to observe), under the circumstances it must be considered understandable.

However, Intensive Interaction is not just about crisis management, but is also widely used to tune into and engage with people with whom it is difficult to communicate (see **Appendix 2: Intensive Interaction**).

Not for nothing is autism described as a spectrum, and the variation in presentation refers not only to the severity of autistic features but also to the way the child responds to sensory distress. While William and Alister react to stress with outbursts that culminate in aggression, some children (and adults) immerse themselves in repetitive behaviour, some remove themselves from the source (as they rightly or wrongly perceive it) by hiding their eyes or running away, some self-harm while others shut down or freeze. The common denominator is that these different behaviours are attempts by the individual to defend themselves against what are perceived and experienced by them as life-threatening assaults: in sensorily overloading them we have triggered the body's self-defence system. Quite why this manifests in so many different behavioural ways is more difficult to understand.

Chapter two: All in the mind?

In the beginning

Turning now to the aetiology of autism, just what proportion of this condition is inherited and how much is due to largely unknown factors (idiopathic) is still a matter of debate. What is clear is that there is no single gene for autism. El-Fishawy and State conclude:

'Autism is not a monogenic disorder. In many but not all individual cases it is likely to be a complex genetic disorder that results from simultaneous genetic variations in multiple genes.'[6]

Starting with fertilisation, in the non-spectrum foetus, sperm meets egg, penetrates egg and there is an exchange of genetic material. The fertilised egg cell forms a protective wall around itself to defend against further intrusion and starts to divide. Around seven to eight days later, at the stage of 64 cells, the solid ball (called a blastula) implants into the wall of the mother's uterus. From now on, embryonic cells are on the move. The ball of cells develops a cavity, into which cells from the outside (ectoderm) fold in on themselves to form an inner layer (endoderm). The origami continues: around the third week, a strip of cells in the dorsal ectoderm (the future back) thickens and its edges rise up like parallel mountain ridges, infolding on the valley between them along the entire length of the future head to tail axis, closing and sealing to form the neural tube, eventually giving rise to the spinal cord enclosed by the spine, with the brain stem and brain at the top end.

There are drastic consequences if the neural tube fails to close correctly and this is known to be responsible for spina bifida – but it has also

---

6   El-Fishawy P & State MW (2010) The genetics of autism: key issues, recent findings and clinical
      implications. *Psychiatric Clinics of North America* **33** (1) 83–105.

been reported as being associated with autism triggered by thalidomide. (About five per cent of thalidomide victims have autism, 30% higher than the rate in the general population[7]). In a post-mortem examination, it was found that the brain stem was shorter than would be expected in the non-spectrum brain and two organs were affected. The facial nucleus (which controls the muscles of facial expression) was reduced in size and the superior olive was missing. Described as a relay station, the superior olive is the first major convergence site for auditory information, measuring where the sound source is located[8].

'The medial superior olive is severely disrupted in the autistic brain. Neurons in this region are significantly smaller and rounder than in controls. Moreover, there is a consistent and significant decrease in the number of superior olive neurons in the autistic brain.'[9]

'Critically, this injury could only have occurred 20–24 days after conception, during the early development of the motor neurons of the cranial nerves, those that innervate muscles of the eyes, ears, face, jaws, throat and tongue.'[10]

These authors suggest that while such aspects of autism as hypersensitivity to sound and touch and problems with sleep could be related to defects in the cranial nerves, not all symptoms of autism arise directly from such deficits – but they may be interfering with the subsequent wiring up of other parts of the brain such as the amygdala, since, for example, cranial nerve five (the trigeminal nerve) is known to direct neural effects onto the amygdala[11].

Environmental factors

Nowadays we live in an atmosphere crowded with chemical pollutants. So where and when might environmental factors also influence embryonic development?

---

7   Rodier PM (2000) The early origins of autism. *Scientific American* **282** (2) 56–63.
8   Oliver DL, Beckius GE & Shneiderman A (1995) Axonal projections from the lateral and medial superior olive to the inferior collicus of the cat. *Journal of Comparative Neurology* **360** (1) 17–32.
9   Kulesza RJ Jr, Lukrose R & Stevens LV (2011) Malformation of the human superior olive in autistic spectrum disorders. *Brain Research* 1367 360–71.
10 Rodier PM, Ingram JL, Tisdale B, Nelson S & Romano J (1996) Embryological Origin of autism: developmental anomalies of the cranial nerve motor nuclei. *Journal Comparative Neurology* **370** (2) 247–61.
11 Jennings D (2010) *Finding the Causes of Autism Spectrum Disorders: The trigeminal factor* [online]. Available at: http://tmjcalifornia.com/wp-content/uploads/2011/11/autism_article_210.pdf (accessed January 2014).

In the nucleus of our cells, our inheritable characteristics are carried on chromosomes: spiral threadlike structures made up of nucleic acids and proteins in the form of genes. The gene is the genetic instruction book and it has two roles. The first is as a template for replication. Second, it is responsible for the organisation and functioning of the cell. To do this, the DNA (deoxyribonucleic acid) in the genes acts as a mould to shape the formation of RNA (ribonucleic acid) outside the cell nucleus, which in its turn codes for and creates proteins. 'Although the template function is largely unaffected by environmental pressure, this transcriptional function is highly responsive to environmental factors such as toxicants, virus infections and hormones.'[12] For example, in an area of the USA where samples of water were found to be contaminated by chemicals such as tetrachlorethylene (which has been shown elsewhere to double the incidence of neural tube closure defects), there was a higher than normal percentage of children on the autistic spectrum.

A recent study implicates severe air pollution, with maternal exposure to traffic fumes doubling the chance of having a child with autism, diesel and mercury being at the top of the list of potential pollutants[13]. Critics have pointed out that computer models were used to estimate exposure rather than direct measurements – and also that mothers living in urban areas were more likely to have access to medical resources and therefore more likely to receive a diagnosis.

Damage in the brain stem

Recent post-mortem studies of people on the spectrum and in mutant 'autistic mice models'[14], show a deficit in the number and reduction in size of Purkinje cells (cells that pass on messages concerned with motor regulation and the co-ordination of motor movements), and suggest that this may arise from damage inflicted by toxins (or other, what are known as 'environmental insults'), rather than from abnormal development[15].

These Purkinje cells are part of a transmission system that relays signals from the sensory organs to the cerebellum (the centre of co-ordination

---

12 London EA (2000) The environment as an aetiological factor in autism: a new direction for research. *Environmental Health Perspectives* 108 (Suppl 3) 401–404.

13 Devlin H (2013) Severe air pollution 'can double risk of having autistic child'. *The Times* **19 June**.

14 Tsai PT, Hull C, Greene-Colozzi E, Sadowski AR, Leech JM, Steinberg J, Crawley JN, Regehr WG & Sahin M (2012) Autistic like behaviour and cerebellar dysfunction in Purkinje cell Tsc1 mutant mice. *Nature* **488** (7413) 647–51.

15 Kern J & Jones A (2006) Study outlining evidence linking autism to cell damage caused by toxic exposure. *Autism Research Review International* **20** (4).

of complex movements using inputs from hearing, balance, visual and muscular systems, as well as executive demands and emotional states[16]). They are activated by picking up messages from climbing cells rooted in the inferior olive. The suggestion is that where there is loss, there are simply not enough Purkinje cells to go round[17]. The effect is that, whereas in the undamaged state, one climbing fibre would be carrying a 'visual input' or a 'sound input', where there is a shortage of Purkinje cells, different messages are getting mixed up in the scramble to hand on signals.

Early investigations suggested that this reduced number of Purkinje cells might be a common factor for all individuals with autism[18] but a more recent study, using a different and more effective staining technique (which the authors say is picking up more of the stained cells), found this reduction in only half the autistic brains that were examined[19].

However, where this loss is evident, a reduction in number of these vital cells – and consequent competition between those that remain – means that there may be insufficient to pick up all the messages that are getting through from the inferior olive, so that incoming visual and auditory stimuli may be forced to end up travelling the same route.

If we imagine the brain as a goods yard, at this stage in some people with autism some of the afferent (incoming) track is missing, so trains from other lines are diverted onto those that remain. More stimuli being fed in than the Purkinje 'conduit' can handle may provide just the sort of sensory overload, confusion and interference that Donna Williams describes when she writes about an environment 'full of static and sparklers and it takes a lot of mental effort and energy to process what I am seeing and hearing'.

(I visited William again today and he showed me a drawing of his 'upgraded anger box'. I ask him why his anger box is now decorated with stars: somehow it seems unlikely. He tells me that when he gets upset he sees 'sort of pinpoint flashes of light'.)

---

16 Unknown (2013) *Brain Differences in Autism: 1 – the cerebellum* [online]. Available at: http://www.saras-autism-diet.freeservers.com/Literature/Brain-001.html (accessed January 2014).

17 Kern JK & Jones AM (2006) Evidence of toxicity, oxidative stress, and neuronal insult in autism. *Journal of Toxicology and Environmental Health. Part B: critical reviews* **9** (6) 485–499.

18 Ritvo ER, Freeman BJ, Scheibel AB, Duong T, Robinson H, Guthrie D & Ritvo A (1986) Lower Purkinje cell counts in the cerebella of four autistic subjects: initial findings of the UCLA-NSAC Autopsy Research Report. *American Journal of Psychiatry* **143** (7) 862–6.

19 Whitney ER, Kemper TL, Bauman ML, Rosene DL & Blatt GJ (2008) Cerebellar Purkinje cells are reduced in a subpopulation of autistic brains. *Cerebellum* **7** (3) 406–416.

It is becoming increasingly clear that autism is unlikely to have a single cause, but that whatever the cause is, it is inbuilt at a very early stage of gestation. Miller and Stromland have associated the absence of at least one particular gene, HOXA1 (which modifies the activities of other genes) with developmental failures at this key stage, around three to four weeks when the cranial nerves are in the process of formation[20, 21].

It is easy to get entangled in the thickets of genetic fragility, chemical imbalance, structural abnormalities and environmental factors, but there does appear to be the beginnings of a trail, one that starts with genetic fragility at the time of fertilisation (and/or possible environmental factors encountered either before fertilisation or in the immediate days following), leading in some cases to failure to close the neural tube, which in its turn effects development of the cranial nerves, not just in themselves but in the part they play in further development of brain structures.

Speculation or hypothesis, it is tempting to select the pieces of information that promote a coherent story. But what all researchers agree is that the situation is extremely complex and global in its effects. At the very least however, emerging evidence focuses our attention on the early organic aetiology of autism, one that affects multiple structures. Although research is necessarily difficult and samples small, results do point to deficits built in when the genetic material in the sperm and egg first come together and divide, either inherited or incorporated shortly after fertilisation.

Inside and outside

One of the problems the non-spectrum world has in understanding the world of autism is that we look at it from our own point of view, focusing on 'behaviours' that strike us as 'bizarre', socially unacceptable or even threatening, forgetting that a so-called 'behaviour' is the outward sign of an inward experience. In a personal account of her own autism, 'WeirdGirlCyndi' is explicit about the relationship between what is happening inside her at the times when she appears to the non-spectrum world to be having a 'tantrum'. A little confusingly, Cyndi uses the term 'sensory overload' in this film[22] to describe what is more properly called an 'autonomic storm' (which I shall refer to later), which is the consequence of sensory overload.

---

20 Stromland K, Nordin V, Miller M, Akerstrom B & Gilberg C (1994) Autism in thalidomide embryopathy: a population study. *Develpmental Medicine and Child Neurology* **36** (4) 351–356.
21 Miller TM, Stromland K, Ventura L, Johansson M, Bandim JM & Gilberg C (2004) Autism with opthalmologic malformations. *Transactions of the American Ophthalmological Society* **102** 107–122.
22 WeirdGirlCyndi (2007) *Sensory Overload Simulation* [online]. Available at: www.youtube.com/watch?v=BPDTEuotHe0 (accessed January 2014).

She says that she is sick of 'so-called experts' trying to explain what they think an autistic person is going through[23]. They think they can 'fix' autistic children by forcing them to 'act normal'. She asks us to watch her video and think how anybody can act normally when they're going through what she simulates as her sensory experience when her brain is tipping into overload. She describes for us what happens if she has to watch a film in a crowded room: the voices sound four times louder than normal and what she sees swirls, zooms and pixelates.

'My brain processes slower. I can't filter out the distractions like voices and noise. If I don't remove myself from the situation immediately I go into sensory overload. To someone watching, I appear to cop an attitude or fly into a rage. Pretty scary and confusing. When I am in overload I'm in a fight or flight response. Acting angry is a defence mechanism like my brain can scare off the source of over-stimulation. Once I am in full overload there is nothing I can do except ride the meltdown until I've expelled all the energy. I just kinda lose my head and explode and then I'm fine.'

In this chapter I want to focus on what it is that is happening inside the brain that is having such dramatic behavioural consequences.

Innervation of the brain

With recent advances in neurology and technological improvements in scanning, attention is turning more and more to getting an accurate picture of the early pathways of embryogenesis in children who subsequently develop autism. What is happening around the time of fertilisation and how does this influence the subsequent development of neural pathways? And what part do environmental factors play?

In her recent book, *The Autistic Brain*, Temple Grandin[24] points out that at the time of its publication, there were 20,000 neurological functional magnetic resonance imaging (fMRI) peer reviewed studies of the brain and these were rising at the rate of eight per day. What is becoming increasingly clear is that, while the nervous system in the brains of those with autism experiences developmental variations, the effect of these dissimilarities

---

23 The antagonistic tone of this comment on 'the experts' may feel uncomfortable to those who are working towards supporting those on the spectrum, but it is echoed through quite a wide swathe of individuals who experience society's attempts to 'normalise' them as invasive (see Chapter 8: A Behavioural Approach).

24 Grandin T & Panek R (2013) *The Autistic Brain*. Boston, MA: Houghton, Mifflin and Harcourt (p23).

varies enormously in different individuals, so that there does not appear to be one 'autistic brain'.

This is put very simply by a boy with autism, who says that his brain is 'not wired up properly' – and it is clear that responses to the same stimulus by people on the spectrum differ from those who are non-spectrum[25]. But, as already mentioned, they also differ within the spectrum. For example, the word 'autism' was chosen to signify aloneness, and yet there are children who are on the spectrum who we are told cannot be autistic since they appear to want cuddles and actively seek physical contact. It is a truism to say that there are as many varieties of autism as there are individuals who have it.

Returning to the image of the brain as an immense goods yard, with nerves coming and going in all directions, the same fibre bundle (for example, the trigeminal nerve) may be carrying messages to the brain (afferent) and from the brain to their destination (efferent). Starting with the numbers of nerve cells (neurons), the figures involved are astronomical – most estimates are of around a hundred billion neurons[26]. In both autistic and non-spectrum brains, most neurons consist of a cell body containing the nucleus, with lots of fine branching arms called dendrites and a single extending leg called an axon.

To pass on information, an electrical charge called an action potential leaves the cell body of a neuron and travels down its axon towards the dendrites of the target cell. Critically, donor and recipient cells do not actually touch each other, being separated by a gap known as the synapse. Information is piggy-backed from one cell to another across the synaptic gap by chemicals known as neurotransmitters.

Transmission of signals across the synapses is immensely complicated and any attempt to describe it is riddled with exceptions. Very roughly speaking, however, when a spike or action potential arrives at the terminus of the axon, it releases a neurotransmitter from a vesicle which diffuses across the synaptic cleft and binds to a receptor site on the dendrites of the post-synaptic, or target, cell.

There are, however, a great many neurotransmitters, each of which has a different property. Normally classified by their chemical structure, most are

---

25 I have used Donna William's term 'non-spectrum' throughout in preference to 'neurotypical', as it is less cumbersome and its meaning is more obvious.

26 Anne Lynn S, Chang H, Katz LM & Piotrowski NA (2007) *Magill's Medical Guide Revised Edition*. Ipswich, MA: Salem Press.

either stimulatory or inhibitory, setting off or damping down excitability. If there is sufficient input it will fire off an action potential in the target cell. In this delicately balanced exchange it is not too difficult to suppose that if one neurotransmitter is out of balance, the whole system gets thrown into turmoil.

Fragile X and the role of neurotransmitters

Studies in the gene responsible for Fragile X Syndrome in autism[27] concern a single neurotransmitter called glutamate. Glutamate is an excitory transmitter that is involved in passing messages from the ears to the medial superior olive, which locates the direction, left or right, of incoming sound. Investigations into the levels of glutamate in people with Fragile X indicate an excess of this amino acid at the synapses[28]. Using mice as models, drugs are being developed to dampen the level of glutamate to reduce the level of over-excitation, and hopefully the sensations of being overwhelmed by sensory stimuli. There are indications that the effects may also apply to humans.

At this stage, the debate surrounding the definition of what represents true autism surfaces: is the autistic-like presentation of individuals with Fragile X the same as that of 'true' autism (something that has been disputed), so that it can represent a valid model for investigation of the genetic fragilities of autism?

Hagerman and her team[29] argue that although not all children with Fragile X are on the spectrum, those that are fully meet the diagnostic criteria for autism.

Looking at it this way round, about 30% of children with Fragile X do have autism as defined by the diagnostic criteria, DSM-1V-TR. A further 20% show developmental disorders as yet unspecified. Hagerman believes that autism and autism spectrum disorders are part of the behavioural phenotype of Fragile X Syndrome and therefore studies of the Fragile X gene do provide a well-founded model for investigations into the aetiology

---

27 Katsnelson A (2012) The autism pill. *Scientific American* **307** (5).
28 Dolen G, Carpenter RL, Ocain TD & Bear BF (2010) Mechanism based approaches to treating Fragile X. *Pharmacology and Therapeutics* **127** 78–93.
29 Hagerman RJ, Rivera SM & Hagerman PJ (2008) The Fragile X family of disorders: a model for autism and targeted treatments. *Current Pediatric Reviews* **4** 40–52.

of autism. They go on to stress that the expansion mutations[30] of the FMR1 gene (the gene responsible for Fragile X) constitute a leading cause of autism, both in terms of the extremely high association between the Fragile X mutation and autism, and by virtue of the fact that the autism of Fragile X satisfies the diagnostic criteria. Hagerman concludes that the study of Fragile X syndrome constitutes a reliable genetic paradigm for the study of common molecular pathways leading to all forms of autism. The implications of Hagerman's research are that what we are calling autism involves an imbalance of neurotransmitters at the synapse and that this is built in at conception.[31]

The autism jigsaw

If axons and neurotransmitters represent the bricks and mortar of the brain, we also need to consider an unusual architecture. Temple Grandin[32] discusses the 'superhighways' that convey information from one processing part of the brain to another, for example, from visual processing to auditory processing areas. She introduces a fascinating hypothesis arising out of work using a new scanning technology, HDFT (high definition fibre tracking)[33], which is able to track fibres through the brain. He suggests that where there is a developmental deficit in one area, the growing brain may try and compensate in another. So whereas, for example, in Temple's brain, there was a deficit in the area of speech organisation, the fibres, needing to grow somewhere, grew into the area of her visual processing. HDFT scans of her brain actually show the lack of fibres in the one area and extra fibres in the other, an imbalance which coincides with her amazing capacity to think in pictures, coupled with difficulties she experienced in developing speech.

It's not only autism itself that is like a jigsaw in terms of what we see, but also what we know about autism in terms of what we do not see. We view its completed face on the cover of the box (how it presents to us in terms of diagnostic criteria and the difficulties we have in finding ways to engage with people on the spectrum and to reduce their evident

---

30 An expansion mutation in a gene is when a short sequence of DNA is repeated, in this case adding a series of the amino acid glutamine to the resulting protein, causing the resulting protein to function improperly.

31 Hagerman RJ, Rivera SM & Hagerman PJ (2008) The Fragile X family of disorders: a model for autism and targeted treatments. *Current Pediatric Reviews* **4** 40–52.

32 Grandin T & Panek R (2013) *The Autistic Brain*. Boston, MA: Houghton, Mifflin and Harcourt (p23).

33 Shin SS, Verstynen T, Pathak S, Jarbo K, Hricik AJ, Maserati M, Beers SR, Puccio AM, Boada FE, Okonkwo DO & Schneider W (2012) High-definition fiber tracking for assessment of neurological deficit in a case of traumatic brain injury: finding, visualizing, and interpreting small sites of damage. *Journal of Neurosurgery* **116** (5) 1062–1069.

anxiety and sometimes bizarre behaviour), but inside the box there are innumerable upside-down pieces waiting to be fitted together. We turn them over, looking for patterns, grasping for clues in the multitude of journals generated by diverse disciplines:

'Each researcher – through the lens of his or her discipline – feels one part of the puzzle and assumes that one or another represents the whole.'[34]

And for the enquirer, not all the relevant information is in journals that are obviously related to autism, and may therefore be overlooked. For example, emerging clues linking cranial pain in autism to trigeminal neuralgia (TN) may appear in dental journals[35], since dentists are the first port of call for those with pain in the jaw. One of the questions I want to ask in this book is to what extent it is possible to link the superabundance of information now becoming available to the experiences of individuals on the spectrum. This is particularly so because of the anxiety and severe pain that some of them describe, since it is easy to misread a behaviour that is consequent on sensory deficits[36] or neurological distortions as 'just part of the autism', a process that can lead to diagnostic overshadowing.

Trigeminal neuralgia?

The non-autistic world still describes autism in terms of how a person reacts. For example, the Triad of Impairments focuses on physical symptoms: the inability to interact, coupled with both a deficit in communication and in social imagination. Subsequently, this categorisation was modified by the designers of the DSM-IV or the DSM-V (and ICD-10): 'The DSM instead introduced repetitive behaviour patterns, not the impaired social imagination, as the last leg of the triad'[37]. However the list of symptoms is presented, it directs our attention to consequence rather than provenance; symptoms rather than cause: how we should deal with such a situation? This is like sandbagging the door against flood

---

34 Yip J, Davis S & Wendt O (2011) Connecting electroencephalography profiles with Gamma-Amino-Butyric Acid (GABA) neuropathology of autisms: a prelude to treatment in mental and behavioural disorders and diseases of the nervous system. In: V Eapen (Ed) *Autism: A neurodevelopmental journey from genes to behaviour*. Rijeka, Croatia: InTech.

35 Jennings D (2010) *Finding the Causes of Autism Spectrum Disorders: The trigeminal factor* [online]. Available at: http://tmjcalifornia.com/wp-content/uploads/2011/11/autism_article_210.pdf (accessed January 2014).

36 Kiani R & Miller H (2010) Sensory impairment and intellectual disability. *Advances in Psychiatric Treatment* **16** 228–235.

37 Wing L & Gould J (1979) Severe impairments of social interaction and associated abnormalities in children: epidemiology and classification. *Journal of Autism and Developmental Disorders* **9** (1) 11–29.

rather than focusing our attention on deforestation in the catchment area. The questions we should be asking are why does the child do this, and what is it that underpins this behaviour?

Take facial pain. My attention was drawn to this by an unusual description by Gunilla Gerland in her fascinating autobiography, *A Real Person*[38]. Extreme sensitivity in her teeth led her to swallow her food without chewing, a habit that her parents tried in vain to correct. On the other hand she describes how she experienced acute pain in her jaw that was actually relieved by chewing substances with a certain consistency. Since her pain was unrelated to dental decay, another possible trigger was Branch 3 of the trigeminal nerve, which runs down the jaw behind the teeth.

'The chewing surface of my teeth was incredibly sensitive to touch – almost electric – and seemed to be connected in some way to a sensitive place in the back of my neck. This could be unbearable and it helped to bite into something – preferably something fairly resistant to the teeth – then the pressure in my mouth evened up. Human flesh was the best of all to bite into: when my sister was feeling kind she would allow me to chew her arm. Mostly I had to be content with things made of soft plastic – my old teething ring, toys, furniture. Whenever I needed to calm that unpleasant feeling in my teeth, I bit into whatever was handy.'

She goes on to describe certain other self-applied diversions she developed that relieved the pain, such as switching her focus to a fixation on curves, following the line with her eye and fingers – and sometimes physically pressing the back of her head against the wall.

Richard also chews. He is 17 and on the severe end of the spectrum. He sits in class, totally abstracted, gnawing at large wooden pieces of a jigsaw. I try to enter his world by communicating through his body language but he is uninterested when I join in his activity by myself biting on a piece of puzzle. When I reflect on this, it becomes obvious that the stimulus he is giving himself is pressure, so my offering of visual feedback (however closely related) is unlikely to offer him a stimulus that is significant. Abandoning this approach, I try using vibration to see if I can enhance the pressure input he is giving himself. When his support teacher places a vibration unit on the chair near his head, it instantly gets his attention. Grabbing it, he immediately presses it to the region of his jaw and then moves it to surround his ear. His eyes

---

38 Gerland GA (2003) *A Real Person: Life on the outside.* London: Souvenir Press.

and whole face light up and he grins broadly. This is a sensation that really has meaning for him[39].

Circumstances dictate that I have to meet eight-year-old Ché in a room at a sports centre. It's noisy and the carpet is so optically disturbing that after half an hour my own eyes start dancing and I have to fetch a blanket to cover it so that there is at least somewhere I can look without visual distress. Ché clearly does not want to be with me and in his efforts to get taken away, he is attacking his mother with persistent ferocity, a not unusual strategy for him. Ché chews things and he is hypersensitive to some sounds. He finds it difficult to cope with a number of people and strange places. When he is disturbed he hits the top of his head and shouts he has pain in it: 'It hurts, it hurts'. It occurs to me that he is possibly experiencing TN in Branch 1 of the trigeminal nerve.

TN is normally an inherited condition, occurring throughout the total population (although it can result from injury). When I enquire if TN is in Ché's family it turns out that both his grandmother and great grandfather have the condition and, furthermore, a scan taken when he was very young revealed damage to the trigeminal nerve (cranial nerve five).

---

39 Caldwell P (2010) *Autism and Intensive Interaction*. Training film. London: Jessica Kingsley Publishers.

Figure 2.1: The trigeminal nerve. Branch 1 covers part of the forehead and a squarish area just above the hairline. Branch 2 covers the nasal area and branch 3, the jaw.

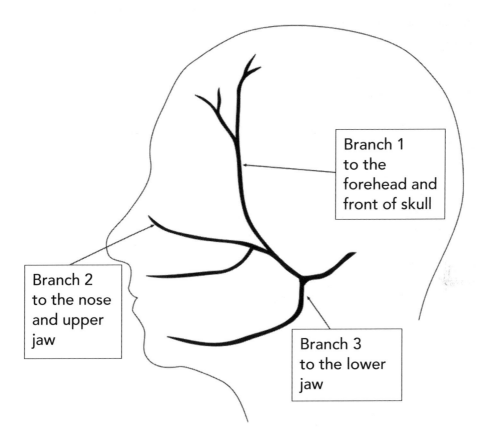

The trigeminal nerve innervates the jaw, nose and front of the upper head. It comes out of the pons, a bulging area of the brain stem in front of the cerebellum and emerges from the skull just behind the ear. It has two functions. The first is sensory, sensing touch, pain and temperature in the face, the second is motor, controlling the muscles used for chewing and mastication.

TN is acute pain in these areas related to the nerve. Its effects can be so devastating that a sufferer may well be self-injuring in an attempt to relieve their distress. It is thought to be caused by compression of the nerve by a nearby blood vessel which would normally be separated from the nerve by a pad of tissue. The myelin sheath is damaged, leading to acute attacks of pain[40]. Where there is reduced physical separation between the blood vessel and the nerve, it would seem reasonable to suggest that when stress activates the sympathetic nervous system during an autonomic storm, with consequent increase in blood pressure, pressure on the nerve increases and triggers the waves of pain. (Medical advice to a colleague whose TN resulted from an accident at the age of 12 was that she should live a life of reduced stress, and she did find this helpful in lowering the incidence of acute attacks[41].)

The acute form described above is the classical presentation of TN. But a factsheet published by a trigeminal nerve support group in the US[42] distinguishes between two different types of the condition.

'Trigeminal neuralgia is a chronic pain condition that affects the trigeminal or 5th cranial nerve, one of the most widely distributed nerves in the head. The typical or "classic" form of the disorder, Trigeminal Neuralgia, "Type I", causes extreme, sporadic, sudden burning or shock-like face pain that lasts anywhere from a few seconds to as long as two minutes per episode. These attacks can occur in quick succession, in volleys lasting an hour to two hours. A second form of TN called "Atypical" or "Type II", is characterized by constant 24/7 aching, burning, boring pain of somewhat lower intensity than Type I. Both forms of pain may occur in the same person, sometimes at the same time.'[43]

In an article in the *British Journal of Anaesthesia*, Nurmikko and Eldridge[44] also make the distinction between typical and atypical types of TN, with the additional subdivision of trigeminal neuropathy. This is particularly interesting from the perspective of autism, since it describes pain as extending beyond the territory of the trigeminal nerve (as described by Donna Williams, William and Gunilla Gerland, where a more generalised

---

40 Okeson JP (2005) *Bell's orofacial pains: the clinical management of orofacial pain.* Quintessence Publishing.
41 Personal communication with author.
42 Living with TN. See http://www.livingwithtn.org/ (accessed January 2014).
43 Attribution: Content of this page is drawn from an article by Richard A "Red" Lawhern, Ph.D, written in June 2012 at the request of the Office of Information at the US National Institute for Neurological Disorders and Stroke (NINDS). This material started out as an update and correction of the NINDS Trigeminal Neuralgia Fact Sheet.
      This pre-publication draft has been reviewed for scope and accuracy by an MD member of the Medical Advisory Board of the US Trigeminal Neuralgia Association. The draft will be taken down and a link provided to the original page at NINDS when they complete internal review and publish the information. However, the information is deemed to be of sufficient importance that we are posting it in pre-publication draft for reference by patients and their physicians
44 Nurmikko TJ & Eldridge PR (2001) *British Journal of Anaesthesia* **87** (1) 117–32.

hypersensitivity of the sympathetic nervous system tracks pain from a central position in the upper chest or nape of the neck, out into the limbs and digits).

Talking about spinal neuralgia, Gunilla Gerland also tells us about two different levels of pain. 'I became slightly used to it but it was a constant torture, most noticeably when it changed in intensity. It was like cold steel down my spine. It was hard and fluid at the same time, with metallic fingers drumming and tickling the outside. Like sharp clips digging in to my spine and lemonade inside. Icy heat and digging, fiery cold. It was like the sound of screeching chalk on a blackboard turned into a silent concentration of feeling, then placed in the back of my neck.'[45]

The intensity of pain can be physically and mentally incapacitating. Judith Bluestone[46], herself with autism, actually suggests the primary defect in autism is a hypersensitivity of the trigeminal nerve: 'When the trigeminal nerve hurts, you can't concentrate on anything else' she says, 'many avoidance behaviours in children with autism are a sign that the trigeminal nerve is distressed.' Like Gunilla, she swallowed her food without chewing it, since in order to feel what her mouth was doing she would have needed to allow herself simultaneously to feel unbearable pain. She adds that, 'many activities, such as face washing, shaving and even speaking, may be translated (by the brain) into pain', a paradox that suggests that under some circumstances the brain may teach itself alternative pathways.

TN can be present on one or both sides of the head. For example, Nicole who has autism and Down's syndrome, is 14. She presses one side of her head, sticks her finger up her nose and presses it in her mouth. She has also recently been diagnosed by her psychiatrist as having TN. Chris, (who we will meet in Chapter 9 and in the postscript), sometimes gets it in one side and sometimes both.

Traditionally, TN has been thought to be rare in children (it is normally diagnosed in non-spectrum people over 50) but the trigeminal nerve factsheet mentioned above[41] suggests that it can occur at any age, including infancy. Although it is not always inherited, the child or niece of a TN patient may have a five per cent chance of presenting with this form of face pain. TN may occur on either side of the face or on both, as mentioned, but

---

45 Gerland GA (2003) *A Real Person: Life on the outside.* London: Souvenir Press.
46 Bluestone J (2004) *The Fabric of Autism.* Bend, OR: The HANDLE Institute.

when the initial presentation includes bilateral pain, the incidence may be higher, perhaps because of an inherited pattern of blood vessel formation.[47]

The connection between autism and TN is therefore confusing. Twenty individuals with TN responded to a query posted on a TN chat-line that although they did not have children with autism, they were themselves diagnosed as having Asperger's syndrome. Particularly interesting (since it appears that just as a diagnosis of autism/Asperger's spectrum can mask TN, so a diagnosis of TN can be camouflaging autism),was the response of a woman who described the difficulties she had in obtaining such a diagnosis. Her TN consultants told her that all her symptoms, her withdrawn state, her need for soft food because eating was painful, her fear of speaking, the need to avoid bright sunshine, were those of TN. It was only when she finally had the operation to correct the TN and the facial pain caused by this was lessened – but her other symptoms persisted – that she was also given a diagnosis of Asperger's.

In view of this, it seems worthwhile asking ourselves to what extent the facial and bodily pain expressed by people with autism is related to damage to the trigeminal nerve, since this underlies a number of behavioural patterns. For example, why are people banging their heads – and how many individuals with autism who are sucking, pulling the hair from the front of their heads, self-harming, biting and chewing or insisting on only eating sloppy food, are doing so in order to relieve facial pain?

Johnny is six years old and on the autistic spectrum. His balance is bad and he prefers to lie on the floor on his back or lounge with his back supported in a chair. He mouths and bites anything and presses his fingers behind his ears. He bangs his head and face.

Johnny is hard to engage because he attacks other children and staff. He is very quick, biting and grabbing and difficult to contain. He tries to push his chin into the face of the child or adult he is attacking and bite. One of the triggers for his attacks is if attention that has been given is withdrawn without warning. He attacks another child as soon as I shift my attention away from him and on to Pete.

Working from the possibility that Johnny may be experiencing head pains of the TN type (which Gunilla Gerland links 'in some way she can't explain to pain in the back of the neck'), I ask his teacher to hold him tight the next time he attacks and rub the back of his neck, exerting very firm pressure.

---

47 See footnote 43.

When she does this, he eases off his attack within a few minutes, whereas normally his outbursts are prolonged. The second time this happens (when I had been working with him through his sounds and had to move on to another child), rubbing the back of his neck had an almost instantaneous effect: his teacher says, 'you can feel him relaxing'. From rigid, his body went slack and he sat down quietly. The storm passed almost as quickly as it had come.

Does Type 2 TN throw light on the number of children on the spectrum who resist having their hair brushed, washed or cut? Compare their behaviours with the personal accounts of the distress caused by their TN offered by non-spectrum individuals:[48]

'I cry when washing or brushing my hair, my scalp feels on fire, like thousands of needles being poked into my head.'

'I apply pressure to the jaw line just below the ear, it does not take away the pain but makes it manageable.'

'I often press on my jaws to relieve the ache. My scalp burns and is very sensitive to touch so brushing my hair and washing it is painful at times.'

'I do hold and press behind my ear at times and doing my hair is just awful! I have a vice gripping pain behind my ear all the time, just the pain level varies.'

'For me it's an all-day thing, there's pressure and that burning feeling your muscles have after you've been running really hard, it's hard to describe. Throughout the day the pain will change and it can feel like anything from my jaw and cheek bone being shattered to teeth being ripped out or someone slicing my flesh on my face.'

'I put off washing my hair as long as possible, gross I know but the water trickling down my face can be a trigger that I'd rather avoid. Talking, chewing, anything in my mouth, a slight breeze, teeth brushing, smiling laughing are all things that can be a trigger. When in a particular bad pain episode I want to be left alone in the dark where's cool, dark and quiet. Because TN can be triggered by social activities such as talking and most people do not want to be around others when in pain you can be anti-social.'

---

48 Online autism chatline (anonymous).

It is important to make clear that it is not being suggested that TN is *always* linked with autism, and where it is, it is not the cause of autism, but rather an effect, or perhaps it would be more accurate to describe it as collateral damage. Where it does exist, however, it can be a trigger to self-harm, or aggression directed at lessening the proximity of the perceived source of the pain.

Let me introduce Amy. In the company of a psychiatrist colleague, I visit her at home at the request of her mother.

Amy is eight. She is diagnosed as having very severe autism and anxiety disorder. She has five siblings. All are either on the spectrum or autism is suspected and awaiting assessment. She is totally fixated on certain short episodes of video (particularly one with children bouncing up and down on a sofa) and she becomes distraught and self-injures if these are not being played continuously. She can rewind the DVD player in her bedroom herself using her toes, so she does not even have to rise and disturb her fixation.

Amy interacts minimally, if at all. She gives little eye contact and almost all the time she is making high-pitched penetrating sounds that escalate to a scream when she is disturbed. Her father says that if he is alone in the house and it is quiet she does respond to her sounds being answered to build up a 'conversation' using her body language. Amy is also trying to say some words, if only fleetingly. She is so disturbed she can only manage an hour a week at school.

She spends much of her day crying, but every four or five hours she screams for around 15 to 20 minutes. After these critical outbursts, which occur apparently for no reason, she is exhausted. When she calms, her face has changed: she is pale, sweaty and clammy and rubs her hand up and down on her nose. Her mother says she looks as if she has been through childbirth. If she does not get what she wants, she beats her head and recently has started to pull out her hair by the roots.

Amy prefers soft food that does not need to be chewed. She appears to be sensitive to light and sound – she hates crowds and loud noises but she is also hyposensitive (under-sensitive) to proprioception (messages from her muscles and joints to her brain telling her what she is doing).

In addition to this, Amy presses her fingers in the angle of her jaw, and behind her ear lobes. She takes hold of and places a vibration unit on her mouth and presses it on the area around her ears. Her teeth have been examined and are not the cause of her distress. She bangs her forehead and is pulling her hair from the front quarter of her scalp just above her forehead, where her hair now looks thin. She rubs her nose. She sucks on a teat and chews. These areas correspond with the regions enervated by branches one, two and three of the trigeminal nerve respectively.

TN is not always easy to diagnose. 'Because of overlapping symptoms, and the large number of conditions that can cause facial pain, obtaining a correct diagnosis is difficult, but finding the cause of the pain is important as the treatments for different types of pain may differ'[49] and 'in the majority of patients the TN is idiopathic and there is no identifiable cause'[50]. While MRI scans may be used to rule out tumour or multiple sclerosis, they 'may or may not clearly show a blood vessel impacting on the nerve'[51]. Medical trials use anticonvulsant medicines such as carbamazepine, which blocks nerve firing, or tricyclic antidepressants to treat pain described as constant, burning or aching.

Amy's father is diagnosed as having TN, and the pain he experiences is so extreme that he bangs his head in order to obtain relief. And although in Amy's case the damage does not show up on her scan, this is not definitive, since it is relieved by amitriptyline, one of the tricyclic antidepressants that relieve pain of the type that TN sufferers experience. Amy has not had a recurrence of her acute episodes since she has been using the amitryptiline, and her mother says that she will occasionally relax sufficiently to interact for up to 15 minutes before needing to take compulsive refuge in her jumping video.

If Amy does have TN, it would appear that she is suffering both Type 2 (the lower level continuous pain) and Type 1 (the extreme version), escalating from one to the other when she is stressed, particularly if she is not able to watch her video of jumping children. Although it may seem far-fetched to the outsider that such awful pain can be held in check by simply watching a video, this is substantiated by another woman with TN who says, 'believe it or not playing games on my nook colour or computer distracts me from the pain. Very rarely does playing games not work.'[52]

---

49 Zakrzewska JM (2002) Diagnosis and differential diagnosis of trigeminal neuralgia. *The Clinical Journal of Pain* **18** 14–21.
50 Office of communications and Public Liason, National Institute of Neurological Disorders and Stroke, National Institutes of Health, Bethseda, MD 20892.
51 Gronseth G, Cruccu G, Alksne J, Argoff C, Brainin M, Burchiel K, Nurmikko T, Zakrzewska JM. Practice Parameter: The diagnostic evaluation and treatment of trigeminal neuralgia (an evidence-based review): report of the Quality Standards Subcommittee of the American Academy of Neurology and the European Federation of Neurological Societies. *Neurology* **71** (15) 1183–90.
52 Online autism chatline (anonymous).

Judith Bluestone's account of her experience of auditory-vestibular distress is fascinating[53], and may share a link with Amy's experience. On the spectrum herself, Judith became deaf by the time she was nine and could presumably no longer receive and therefore react to the sounds she found distressing. When her hearing was surgically restored through fenestration, 'my autistic behaviours ("stims"), intensified – until I learned that I could shut down the stimulation in my inner ear by jumping on a pogo stick'. She continues, 'the inner ear and vestibular system shut down when they experience rapid movement and sudden stops. Spinning, jumping and head banging are all ways to shut down an overwhelmed middle and inner ear system'. Importantly, she says it is the *jerk* that relieved her sensitivity. Ros Blackburn[54] uses a trampoline to provide a similar stimulus. Bearing in mind Amy's fixation on running this particular video and her escalation from low level pain to high level pain when this is not happening, is it possible that in Amy's case simply watching the jerk may be triggering an internal motor equivalent sufficient to hold her attention?

The diagnosis of facial pain is extremely complex and we need to consider the possibility that acute facial and bodily pain associated with damage to the trigeminal nerve (or, less commonly, the facial nerve) is more widespread than has been recognised. Reaching even further back into its aetiology, in an online discussion of clinical evidence, it is suggested that in some cases pain in the trigeminal nerve can result from malignment of the cranio-mandibuar joint, which causes bite abnormalities resulting in sensitisation of the trigeminal nerve, leading eventually to hyperacusis (hypersensitive hearing)[55].

If I have laboured this section it is because nerve-related pain can be the camouflaged partner of autism, underpinning a number of behavioural disturbances, for example, some repetitive behaviours that are an attempt to cut out sensory overload and therefore the danger of tipping in to the autonomic storm.

---

53 Bluestone J (2004) *The Fabric of Autism*. Bend, OR: The HANDLE Institute.
54 For more information about Ros, see www.triangle.org.uk/ (accessed Jan 2014).
55 Jennings D (2010) *Finding the Causes of Autism Spectrum Disorders: The trigeminal factor* [online]. Available at: http://tmjcalifornia.com/wp-content/uploads/2011/11/autism_article_210.pdf (accessed January 2014).

Chapter three: Processing problems

Pain

The pain and confusion experienced by people on the autistic spectrum is extremely complicated, and this applies particularly to pain connected with sound stimuli. To begin with, each person seems to have their own individual auditory profile. In some, the problem will be related to specific high or low frequencies, while in others the exact quality of the trigger is difficult to quantify. For example, Charlene cannot bear the sound of metal cutlery so her family uses plastic knives and forks. For others, the problem is with volume – they can manage quiet voices but not loud – for yet others, the offending noise may be as little as a ball point pen clicking in and out. Yet again, sudden sounds can be a problem even if quiet[56].

To complicate matters, confusion is not always simply a question of a noise or sound as such, but also (as one might expect if processing is competing for restricted access) related to what else in the way of simultaneous inputs are arriving at the same time[57]. Extracting human voice from loud, low frequency background noise may be difficult since the neural regulation of the middle ear muscles may be defective[58]. A very complex but relatively common processing difficulty arises for some individuals when they hear overlapping speech. This is particularly evident in community homes where it is not uncommon for individuals to become distressed during changeover time, when two shifts of support workers are exchanging information.

---

56 Grandin T (2013) *Temple Grandin: An inside view of autism* [online]. Available at: http://www.autism. com/index.php/advocacy_grandin (accessed December 2013).
57 Williams D (1996) *Autism: An inside-out approach*. London: Jessica Kingsley Publishers.
58 Thomas WG, McMurry G & Pillsbury HC (1985) Acoustic reflex abnormalities in behaviourally disturbed and language delayed children. *Laryngoscope* **95** (7 pt1) 811–17.

The link with pain is not always necessarily directly that of hyperacusis, (hypersensitivity to the input itself) but rather that auditory overload, as with any kind of sensory overload, can trigger a sympathetic nervous system over-active response. Thus, Temple Grandin experiences panic attacks when she hears sudden noises, even those which are not necessarily loud.

Processing auditory stimuli

In 'WeirdGirlCyndi's' film[59], the author tells us that she can manage to watch a film while on her own but if people come into the room she can no longer cope with the additional distraction (see p.13). The sounds become a roar (in the film the roar is made up of people talking over each other). Everything breaks up as this extra processing tips her into what she says we call a tantrum. Or, as Donna Williams says, if you put the kettle on, 'eventually the whistle will blow'[60]. Even anticipation of auditory or other sensory overload can create a sense of anxiety about the presence of more than one person, in the sense of fear of future overload and of being placed in positions where this will occur.

When he is walking in the park, Rod will wear ear muffs to protect him from unanticipated loud noises but not when he is at home. However, he is so frightened of normal speech and of the difficulties of processing overlapping speech (which for him is overwhelmingly loud) that he will not allow people to come into the house. When I ring the doorbell, he shouts, 'No, no,' and, waving his arms at me, starts to become very distressed. It was only when I stand still by the door and whisper, 'I will speak very quietly,' that he calms and allows me to enter. I have to reduce his anxiety by letting him know that I have understood his difficulty and I am not going to do something that will cause him pain.

A hypersensitivity to sound can even become associated with an unacceptable individual word[61].

Mike, for example, cannot not bear the word 'move'. When he hears it he becomes completely distraught, breaking up furniture and, in the words of his manager, 'you need a dustpan and brush to sweep up the pieces'. In this case the problem lies not so much with the sound itself but that his brain

---

59 WeirdGirlCyndi (2007) *Sensory Overload Simulation* [online]. Available at: www.youtube.com/watch?v=BPDTEuotHe0 (accessed December 2013).

60 Williams D (1996) *Autism: An inside-out approach*. London: Jessica Kingsley Publishers.

61 Thorpe A, Bess F, Sladen D, Schissel H, Couch S & Schery T (2006) Auditory characteristics of children with autism. *Ear and Hearing* **27** (4) 430–441.

is interpreting this particular word as life-threatening. In an attempt to de-sensitise him I ask his support worker to type 'move' onto his computer screen (a visual rather than an auditory input). By changing the font and font size, he gradually gains a little more control. He begins to talk about it and tells us it is a blasphemous word. Unfortunately, at this stage he is moved away, so we are unable to continue assisting him to come to terms with what is for him, in auditory terms, an extremely traumatic event.

In a way, the term 'hypersensitivity' is misleading, since in some cases cause is being confused with effect. For example, while most references to hypersensitivities to sound are referring to acuity, Donna Williams (to whom we owe so much of what is known about what it feels like to be autistic) uses it in the sense of the brain's affective response to sensory overload caused by any stimulus. 'The underlying causes of hypersensitive reactions,' she says, 'may have nothing to do with the perception of pitch or volume but rather are the result of information processing problems'[62].

In this respect, according to Steiger and Davis[63], there is no empirical evidence that the hearing of people on the spectrum 'differs physiologically from a non-autistic control group'. Gravel *et al*[64] showed that children on the spectrum showed the same sensitivity to hearing as those without autism, a finding that was confirmed by Thorpe[65], despite the evidence of some parents of children on the spectrum, that their children displayed avoidance behaviour when they heard certain sounds.

But still, anecdotal evidence can contradict this: some individuals are directly hypersensitive to sound, although it may not be triggering a stress reaction. Clearly Mark, who has severe autism, does hear much more acutely than those of us who support him. He loves aeroplanes and will start to point to the sky and dance around with pleasure long before anyone else can see or hear the plane that invariably appears in that quarter. It would seem reasonable to say he is truly hypersensitive to sound, he hears more acutely than we do. And a parent on the spectrum tells me that when she is in the kitchen she can hear what her children are saying at the far end of the yard outside sufficiently clearly to be able to join in their conversation.

---

62 Williams D (1996) *Autism: An inside-out approach.* London: Jessica Kingsley Publishers.
63 Steigler LN & Davis R (2011) Managing sound sensitivity in individuals with ASDs. *Audiology.*
64 Gravel J, Dunn M, Lee W & Ellis M (2006) Peripheral audition of children on the autistic spectrum. *Ear and Hearing* **27** (3) 299–312.
65 Thorpe A, Bess F, Sladen D, Schissel H, Couch S & Schery T (2006) Auditory characteristics of children with autism. *Ear and Hearing* **27** (4) 430–441.

The connection between Judith Bluestone's auditory experience, her inner ear, vestibular system and her autism, which was explored on p28, provides a further demonstration – her deafness from the age of nine had a limiting effect on her 'stimming', but when her hearing was restored some years later, this limiting effect was lost and her 'autistic behaviours' intensified.

The next question is whether or not to use ear protection devices to cut out background sounds and so make processing easier, or to look at ways of refocusing attention and retraining the brain so that it can tolerate sounds that it was unable to do previously. And it does seem that in some situations the brain can be retrained even to the point of restructuring. For example, recent work on the ability of ballet dancers to pirouette without becoming dizzy shows that during their rigorous training, the cerebellum (where movement vestibular input is organised) actually shrinks in size[66]. First, however, I want to look at how one can filter out excess stimuli.

Headphones

The new generation of pilots' 'active' headphones, which cut down sound selectively, send out noise cancelling waves reducing ambient background noise by up to 70%, so that pilots can hear each other speak over engine noise. These can be extremely effective for some people on the spectrum[67].

The next three interventions describe the use of BOSE Quiet Comfort 15 Acoustic Noise Reduction headphones to help children cope with overlapping speech which is overloading their systems. (It should be pointed out that these 'active' headphones fulfil a different purpose to passive headphones, which muffle all incoming sound.)

A young man with autism (16) is crouched in a noisy area waiting for a lift home. His hood is up and he is withdrawn into himself. When the fire alarm goes off it obviously hurts and he reacts immediately, sticking his fingers in his ears. I pass him a pair of the headphones. He stands up, his hood comes off, he squares up, walks down the passage and returns grinning broadly, 'Now I can go to college,' he says, 'I couldn't stand the noise and the people before!' Several months on, his headphones have changed his life in that he is successful at college, tolerating a situation that previously threatened to deny him access to further education.

---

66 BBC (2013) *Ballet dancers' brains 'adapt to spins'* [online]. Available at: http://www.bbc.co.uk/go/em/fr/-/news/health-24283709 (accessed December 2013).
67 BOSE Quiet Comfort 15 Noise Cancelling Headphones.

An eight-year-old boy is unable to comply with his teacher. He presents as very anxious. The headphones enable him to understand what he is being taught. Although he does not speak, he can understand and respond through his iPad and he is more relaxed in class.

At lunchtime, Timmy will not sit at the table. He lies down and beats his hands on the floor, shouting, 'I'm so angry, I'm so angry'. Listening to the family chatting to each other over the meal, it is noisy and there is a lot of overlapping speech. However, he can manage to sit with them and eat once he wears the BOSE headphones.

These are just three examples of the number of children with whom I have worked recently who are now able to attend and respond when the overall background noise is reduced. But it is interesting that in reducing ambient noise, it appears to cut down on the general confusion caused by too much input suggesting that there is a limit in the total capacity to process that is not just mode specific.

An alternative approach to using sound cancelling headphones was taken by a consultant audiologist, Michael Brown[68]. Addressing the problems of a man who became extremely disturbed when he heard certain sounds, Brown measured the frequencies of these sounds and made a hearing aid mould. He drilled a hole in the mould and filled it with an acoustic material that specifically cut out the frequencies that were so disturbing his patient. The man's so-called challenging behaviour stopped at once; it had simply been a response to unbearable pain. (For those who want to try out this approach, I am assured that this is a technique within the competence of any good music technician.)

The question has been raised as to whether using headphones or other blocking aids is counterproductive, in that the brain may 'give up' and cease the struggle to make sense of incoming auditory signals[69]. For instance, there is evidence that 'the habitual use of ear-muffs may exacerbate sound sensitivities over time'. 'If the ears are not appropriately challenged and are instead routinely shielded from challenging environmental sounds, sensitivity thresholds might go down'[70]. However, the ear muffs used in this research were passive, 'Outdoor Kids Ear Muffs' and the author goes on to say, 'these sound isolators have non-specific broadband sound attenuating

68 Brown M (undated) Audiology Department, Lancaster Royal Infirmary (now retired). Private Seminar.
69 Steigler LN & Davis R (2011) Managing sound sensitivity in individuals with ASDs. *Audiology*.
70 Jastrboff PJ & Hazell JWP (2008) *Tinnitus Retraining Therapy-Implementing the Neurophysiological Model*. Cambridge: Cambridge University Press.

characteristics. As a result, they muffle many kinds of sounds across a wide continuum of frequencies. Speech sounds are reduced presenting a barrier to communication and so can engender social isolation'[71].

It is difficult to sustain this objection to the use of the BOSE headphones since recent advances in acoustic noise reduction headphones such as BOSE are selective rather than global, only cutting down background noise, making it easier to process and hear local speech. (Even if they do not cut all background noise completely, they take the edge off the more penetrating input.)

Nevertheless, if blocking out sound is felt to be a danger, can the brain be helped by auditory desensitisation?

Auditory desensitisation

On an anecdotal level, a mother describes in detail how she is able to help her autistic children come to terms with ambient sound by very gradually turning up the level of the radio in minute increments over several months[72].

Retraining the brain in people with autism comes mainly in the form of Auditory Integration Training (AIT) – an educational programme using targeted music in which some of the low and high frequencies have been removed, devised by Berard[73], an ear, nose and throat consultant, to help retrain the auditory system. There are claims and counterclaims for its success, mainly centring around what is actually being assessed and the methods of doing so. The training is expensive and an up-to-date report in Research Autism[74] concludes that AIT is unhelpful in improving symptoms of autism (which may not be grounded in hypersensitivity to sound but rather relate to processing problems), although it may be of limited use in helping with sensory problems such as hyperacusis. In a blind test, measuring improvement by behavioural changes, parents were unable to say if their children had participated in the training[75].

---

71 Morris R (2009) *Managing Sound Sensitivity in Autistic Spectrum Disorder. New Technologies for Customised Intervention* [online]. Cambridge, MA: Massachusetts Institute of Technology. Available at: http://affect.media.mit.edu/pdfs/09.Morris-thesis.pdf (accessed January 2014).

72 Morris R (2003) *Managing Sound Sensitivity in Autism Spectrum Disorder: New technologies for customised intervention*. Princeton, NJ: Princeton University.

73 Berard G (1997) Auditory integration training (Berard's Method). In: NAS (Eds) *Approaches to Autism, 3rd Edition*. London, National Autistic Society.

74 Research Autism (2013) *Auditory Integration Training and Autism* [online]. Available at: http://researchautism.net/autism_treatments_therapies_intervention.ikml?print&ra=4 (accessed January 2014).

75 Mudford OC, Cross BA, Breen S, Cullen C, Gould J & Douglas J (2000) Auditory integration training for children with autism: no behavioural benefits detected. *American Journal on Mental Retardation* **105** (2) 118–129.

So, if we are to believe that children with autism do not on the whole have more acute hearing than non-spectrum children, then we have to look elsewhere for their very evident distress when confronted with the sounds and noises they find so disturbing. As Williams points out, the problem is not with the sounds themselves but the stress involved in trying to interpret the overloaded system, in making meaning from what has been heard (or seen, in the case of visual distortion)[76]. Recent research suggests that impaired audition stems from complex neural deficits rather than outer ear dysfunction[77]. In the next chapter we shall consider if the problem is not originating directly from the ear, where the very evident pain is coming from.

If I prick my finger, my finger tells me it is hurting and suggests I take steps to pull the splinter out of my flesh. But this is an incorrect reading: what has happened is that my finger has fast-tracked a message to my brain and it is my brain that is telling me that my finger is hurting and suggests I take immediate remedial action. In actual fact, I am dependent on my brain's interpretation or misinterpretation of a situation as to whether or not I experience a sensation as pain. Importantly, Ceponiene et al[78] suggest that the deficit in responsivity or orientating to sound has more to do with attention than sensory intake processes.

If we take this view, the problem lies not so much in the ears themselves as in where focus is directed. To put it personally, is my brain listening to the trigger sound and processing it as painful, or is it possible to direct my attention elsewhere? Am I hearing a stimulus that triggers anxiety and pain in my brain, which sends me into sensory overload? What am I listening to, the stimulus or the distress, the sound or the inward response?

In this context, while noise cancelling headphones reduce or block the trigger, an alternative that is sometimes successful is distraction, which can relate to the context of presentation and effects how the brain is able to process the offending stimulus. Experience suggests that the lower the stress level the more likely the person is to be able to process it successfully.

Pranve is apparently hypersensitive to sound. Living on the edge of Heathrow runway he is highly distressed, attacking his mother frequently.

---

76 Williams D (1996) *Autism: An inside-out approach*. London: Jessica Kingsley Publishers.
77 Davis R & Steigler LN (2005) Towards more effective audiological assessment of children with autistic spectrum disorder. *Seminars in Hearing* **26** (4) 241–252.
78 Ceponiene R, Lepisto T, Shestakova A, Vanhala R, Alku P, Naatanen R & Yaguchi K (2003) Speech-sound-selective auditory impairment in children with autism: they can perceive but do not attend. *Proceedings of the National Academy of Sciences* **100** 5567–5572.

His behaviour has led to his being excluded from a number of day centres. Every time an aeroplane comes in to land he lifts his head in anxiety, it obviously hurts him. However, when I engage with him using his body language (see **Appendix 2: Intensive Interaction**), he visibly relaxes and after 20 minutes of interaction he has ceased looking up when planes pass over. His attention is now redirected outwardly to the mutual (and fascinating) non-verbal 'conversation' we have developed using his movements, rhythms and sounds. As his focus is distracted from his brain's interpretation of the high-pitched whine of the planes as pain, he visibly relaxes and makes no attempt to attack me.

A child who cannot bear the noise of a toilet flushing (so will not use the toilet) but loves horses, is reconciled to the sound when her mother pastes a large picture of a horse's head on the cistern. And, as Jackson and King have shown[79], the context can be important: children who disliked the sound of the toilet flushing could tolerate it if it was played on an audiotape in clinical surroundings.

Each child is different, so registering changes in behaviour to evaluate success is difficult to standardise, unless one accepts that these will relate to the child's individual behavioural baseline. In the following intervention, two children in their classroom are physically blocking out sound – but Davy is switching off: his brain has simply learned to shut out what he finds intolerable.

Davy is eight and non-verbal. I am asked to visit him at school. I have seen him once before and noted that he responded much better when I spoke to him in a whispered voice. He and five other children are sitting in a row in front of the TV watching a noisy cartoon. Two of the children have their fingers in their ears but Davy is completely lost in his own world. He gets up and wanders around vaguely. When I ask his new teacher if I may try the headphones on him, she points to the two others who are obviously cutting out sound but remarks that she does not think that hypersensitivity to sound is Davy's problem. So first we try the headphones on the two children with their fingers in their ears. Both sit up and take notice and we have difficulty in retrieving them. We then try them on Davy, who puts them on his head and takes them off again after a minute or so. He then voluntarily puts them on again and, with a look of interest on his face, lifts the earpiece away from his ear and replaces it carefully each time. His

---

79   Jackson H & King N (1982) The therapeutic management of an autistic child's phobia using laughter as the anxiety inhibitor. *Behavioural Psychotherapy* **10** 364–369.

support worker wrongly suggests he is playing with them – but Davy is an intelligent child and what he is actually doing is testing their effect.

We met Ché in the last chapter (p.20) in a discussion on TN. Ché was hitting his head and crying that it hurt: he was clearly distraught. In order to try and reduce his stress levels, I suggest that his mother tried the BOSE headphones to see if reducing his sensory overload would make his life easier. She emailed me the following week:

'Ché takes the headphones to nursery school with him, they said at times when noise level is high he will ask for them, then will stay calmer than usual at these times. School have also noticed a difference in that he is now trying to form some sort of relationships with peers, although this is causing other problems! As a family we can, although not much, go into a shop etc if Ché wears his headphones and he seems to try and bolt less.'

A few months later, Ché takes his headphones to school and they are placed where they are accessible to him – he knows where they are. But now it seems that simply being able to have them any time he wants them has reduced his anxiety and this has had a knock-on effect on his hypersensitivity.

The alternatives, therefore, seem to be blocking (reducing the source of the pain), distraction (refocusing the brain's attention on what it regards as a more interesting activity) and desensitisation (teaching the brain to recognise that the trigger signal is not pain). Judith Bluestone describes how, as she grew older, she actually managed to teach herself that the noise of her own chewing, which she experienced as pain, was in fact sound.

On the other hand, Temple Grandin[80] says that 'while she has learned to live with the sounds of air hand dryers and alarms, for some people their sensory problems are so debilitating that they cannot function in normal environments like offices and restaurants. Pain or confusion define their lives.'

From a practical point of view, what needs to be uppermost is simple: which approach works for this child? If the child will tolerate the BOSE headphones, this is the most direct intervention, the one that reduces anxiety and pain and allows a child (or adult) to maintain their place within education or whatever their circumstances – otherwise there is a severe danger that he or she will be under-performing or stressed out and in some cases written off as ineducable. Noise selective headphones do not

---

80 Grandin T & Panek R (2013) *The Autistic Brain*. Boston, MA: Houghton, Mifflin and Harcourt.

cut out all the sound, so the individual still has to listen, they simply reduce the background noise that clogs up the processing system.

Even if the use of headphones does produce alterations in sound sensitivity, it may be expedient to use them in the interests of reducing sensory distress and the advantages obtained by continuing education and social equilibrium. On balance, they would seem to be worth trying: even if they are worn only in school it gives the child a chance to attend class and keep up with their peers.

Chapter four:
Seeing straight

Visual distortions

Just as the use of selective headphones may allow a child with auditory processing problems to operate more effectively, so also does the following account of visual distortions draw attention to the need to look at other sensory limitations relevant to autism. In the following story, it becomes evident that we cannot accurately judge the intellectual capability of a child until we have addressed what are, in the fullest sense of the word, physical handicaps.

Mike is in his teens and is in the class for slow learners at his special school. I notice that he squints when he looks out of the window and suggest to his mother that he needs a colourimetric test to see if he has Irlen syndrome. This condition, one that affects the non-spectrum population as well as those with autism, does not show up in a normal eye test since it is a processing rather than a visual problem (one that is triggered by bright light, certain colours or patterns), but is relatively common in autism and can be critical in making sense of what is going on in the environment. Unable to filter out input that is unimportant, visual intake is distorted and can appear as a swirling, zooming and pixillating mass. Objects may be floating and break up. Nothing is stationary, everything is on the move.

An Irlen colourimetric test showed that Mike did indeed have visual processing problems (as well as short sight in his left eye), and he was prescribed blue-tinted lenses. The outcome of his wearing these was dramatic and, with his permission, I quote from his emails to me verbatim:

'I have my tinted lenses... I thought everyone's eyesight was the same as mine. When I put them on for the first time I was seriously disorientated but soon adjusted, they've made a massive difference in my eyesight and when I go outside I don't squint my eyes half as much now. I have also noticed a difference at school now with my glasses. I haven't been as anxious about school and my panic attacks are a lot better.'

A few weeks later:

'The glasses have made a brilliant difference and teachers cant keep up with me at school and i have been put on a gifted and talented list since i got the glasses. when i take them off at night i still cant believe how bad my eye sight was.' (*sic*)

Subsequently, Mike had to be moved to a school that could cater for his high level of intelligence, since he was clearly misplaced in his special school. Naturally he had had a lot of catching up to do, since until his visual distortions were corrected he was missing out on most of what was going on around him. But what is critical is that we cannot tell how able a child is until we have paid attention to and, where possible, corrected their sensory deficits.

At a recent training day, a teacher tells me that she had been informed that Irlen lenses do not work. And in general, current discussion of their effectiveness in improving reading in children with dyslexia ranges from scepticism and disbelief[81] to (as for Mike) grateful experience. The problem is that almost all the evidence is anecdotal rather than empirical – and most research papers are currently not independently peer reviewed, or remain as unpublished theses. Further research investigations face the difficulty of an adopted stance of confidentiality written into training contracts. And since the method of testing is designed for people with dyslexia, it is not always appropriate for those on the spectrum.

Irlen testing is conducted by a qualified diagnostician who uses a colorimeter to determine the colour of a lens that will allow the individual to interact most effectively with their environment, or by a qualified screener who uses colour overlays to see which tint allows a dyslexic individual to read most easily. Both approaches require considerable co-operation on the part of those being tested, demands that a person with autism may find 'threatening' (being in a strange place under strange

81 McIntosh RD & Ritchie JJ (2012) Rose-tinted? The use of coloured lenses to treat Reading Difficulties. In DS Sergio and M Anderson (Eds) *Neuroscience in Education: The Good, the Bad and the Ugly*. Oxford: Oxford University Press.

circumstances), or it may be intellectually beyond their capacity to respond appropriately if they also have a learning disability.

As with auditory testing, light distortions apparently also arise from a number of different triggers and it is not always clear exactly what exactly is being tested. The child or adult's visual problems may stem from colour responses, in which case the environment will be perceived more clearly (and therefore responded to more accurately) through a specific coloured lens. Some difficulties require measurement of the depth of the tint (saturation) but some relate to light intensity, in which case attenuating the strength of light with grey sunglasses, or using dimmer switches or concealed light sources may be helpful. And yet others are responsive to both colour and intensity. Even white light is not just white light but is made up of different light frequencies. And as with sound, the ability to process visual information is also affected by the level of anxiety the person is experiencing[82, 83].

Temple Grandin[84] tells us that autistic people 'get visual cues mixed up with aural ones'[85]. 'When autistics are listening to sound cues, their visual cortices remained more active than neurotypicals.' If that is the case, then even while they are straining to process aural cues, they're being distracted and confused by visual ones.

In this context, if we consider the competition for a reduced number of Purkinje cells available to transport visual and auditory information into the cerebellum in some people on the autistic spectrum, it is not surprising when Donna Williams tells us that she can hear better if she is wearing her coloured lenses – suggesting that the actual capacity to process auditory and visual stimuli appear to intermingle, with consequent interference and distortions. It is just the sort of bottleneck one might expect.

Irlen syndrome

Demand for coloured lenses by those with autism grew from people like Donna who realised that it was not only letters or digits that were jumping around, but, for them, all their environment was behaving like a runaway kaleidoscope. When she first put her tinted glasses on, she tells us the whole world went 'shunt' and she realised, 'oh my God, that's what the

---

82 Cowan J (undated) Personal communication with author.
83 Theobald GN (undated) Personal communication with author.
84 Grandin T & Panek R (2013) *The Autistic Brain*. Boston, MA: Houghton, Mifflin and Harcourt.
85 Sanchez S (2011) *Functional Connectivity of Sensory Systems in Autism Spectrum Disorders: An fcMRI study of audio-visual processing* [online]. San Diego: San Diego State University. Available at: http://sdsu-dspace.calstate.edu/handle/10211.10/1760 (accessed January 2014).

rest of the world is seeing'. When she took them off, everything slid away again. She makes it clear that what she is experiencing is a purely physical effect. A similar effect was noted in a non-verbal man who appeared to be adversely affected by strong light. He rejected the offer of green lenses, but when given red ones, he raised his head and, open-mouthed, looked round the room in what was clearly amazement.

A colleague (not on the spectrum) who has dyslexia tells me that even for her, when she is subjected to visual stress (in her case, bright or fluorescent light) she gets a hot feeling to her head (she places her hands on either side of her head to show me) and sweats and feels panicky if she does not have her glasses. This used to happen particularly when she was teaching and felt it might cause difficulties for her students if she was wearing dark glasses, since they would be unable to make eye contact. For such circumstances as these she has now developed stress-reducing preventative strategies, such as looking away from the source, looking down – and practicing yoga breathing.

Mike's experience described earlier is particularly interesting, not only for the dramatic effect it has had on his quality of life but also because he is so articulate and consequently able to understand and co-operate with his consultant. However, there are many people on the autistic spectrum who do not have his ability but who could benefit from testing. Even if they cannot tolerate wearing glasses, they may be helped by using coloured light bulbs or altering the colour of their room.

Apart from those who are obviously affected by light that is too intense, there are some who show a clear preference for a room of a certain colour – in my practical experience this has been for a blue or for a neutral greyish willow green, seeking out this room in which they are able to be calm. Or they may be rejecting a certain colour, particularly if it is bright and shiny. An eight-year-old boy could not bear the orange fluorescent tiles surrounding his school sandpit area, another had problems with the brilliant green carpet his mother had bought to cheer up his room. Even these preferences are complicated by the tendency of some individuals to fixate on a certain bright colour, one which does not calm them but drowns out the particular input they are unable to tolerate. In the same way, a child who has problems listening to certain frequencies may hug the drying machine in order hear at least one sound that helps them to make sense of their surroundings. This at least gives them a visual or auditory reference point when the rest of the world is swirling or booming around.

Finally, the visual problem may relate to pattern, to blotches on the carpet, or to superimposed movement in front of pattern. For example, the arrangement of a room where I was giving a talk in a licensed club was such that I was standing in front of the mesh grill pulled down over the bar. For three non-spectrum participants (out of 40), my walking up and down in front of the reticular mesh made them feel sick. We had to hang bin-bags over the counter to neutralise the visual disturbance.

In my book, *Finding Me Finding You*[86], I discuss a number of studies of people with autism whose behaviour is altered when viewing their environment through different tinted lenses or in different coloured rooms, including that of a man whose agitation is markedly reduced when he breaks his prescription lenses and staff lend him a pair of red tinted sunglasses[87]. In a room where the colour could be altered, Diane Pauli tested the behaviour of children when placed in different coloured lights and found a marked reduction in repetitive behaviour in different coloured lighting, for example, green/blue light as opposed to red[88].

In practice, the testing of autistic children or adults who cannot respond to questionnaires, or to queries as to whether or not a particular colour is 'better' or 'worse', depends on recording (sometimes long-term) changes in behaviour, particularly levels of anxiety. Looking at the considerable number of anecdotal reports of improved quality of life and behaviour, there is a clear need for research into the most effective ways of testing people on the less able end of the autistic spectrum.

---

86 Caldwell P (2006) *Finding Me Finding You*. London: Jessica Kingsley Publishers (p43).
87 Therapist at workshop: personal communication with author.
88 Pauli D (2003) Thesis. Birmingham University Education Department.

Chapter five:
Internal messages
to the brain

Peace and quiet

Gail Gillingham[89] addresses the need for people with autism to experience tranquillity in their visual and auditory environment – not always easy to achieve in practice, especially in a society dedicated to living in community. Families are noisy, schools are noisy – particularly at break time and during meals – swimming pools and supermarkets are noisy. The direct link between level of stimulus and the body's response is put simply by Temple Grandin: 'When I hear a sudden noise, I have a panic attack. My heart pounds'[90]. While tinted lenses and active noise reduction headphones may reduce the amount of sensory input that has to be processed (and consequently reduce the strain on the sympathetic nervous system), it is not only external sources that are overloading the brain.

Proprioceptive and vestibular regulation

Again I refer back to Judith Bluestone's experience, related in her interesting book *The Fabric of Autism* and discussed on p28, in which she found that a pogo stick helped her and describes how she became dependent on her jerky progression to calm her, the rapid movement and sudden stops seemingly acting to 'shut down' the inner ear and vestibular system[91].

---

89 Gillingham G (1995) *Autism Handle with Care*. Edmonton, Canada: Tacit Publishing Inc.
90 BBC (2006) The Woman Who Thinks Like a Cow. *Horizon*. BBC2. Archive film.
91 Bluestone J (2005) *The Fabric of Autism*. Bend, OR: The HANDLE Institute.

Ros Blackburn would sympathise with this: in a seminar she said that, even as an adult, she spends her time 'travelling round the country as a speaker in order to earn money to take time to trampoline' – it is pivotal to her ability to maintain calm. Lindsey Weeks[92] says he bangs his head against the wall to stop sensory overload.

Unlike ears or eyes, the vestibular (balance) system, with its three semi-circular canals tucked inside the inner ear and filled with fluid responding to movement by flowing over sensitive cells, is a hidden organ. As such it is frequently overlooked in the search for understanding the sensory distortions characteristic of autism. Its multiple effects on posture, balance and head and eye movements are further complicated by its intimate relationship with proprioception (messaging to the brain from muscles and joints describing their tone and position), all of which combine to tell us of our boundaries, what we are doing and where we are in space.

Donna Williams tells us her compulsive and repetitive spinning, jumping from heights, climbing to great heights and throwing herself off backwards may all have been attempts to develop a vestibular system that wasn't able to work consistently or efficiently[93].

'We don't even have proper control over our bodies. Both staying still and moving when we are told is tricky – it's as if we are remote controlling a robot.'[94]

To compound the way we think about what are known as our haptic senses, common parlance tends to use the same word, 'touch', for both touch (as feeling) and proprioception (touch as pressure), when in fact their sensors are different.

Information from the vestibular system travels directly to the cerebellum through some of its afferent nerves: together they modulate the motor pathways that control balance and gaze[95, 96]. However, sensory integration is complex and in practice it can be extremely difficult to work out exactly where any hyper- and hypo-sensitivities are acting, which part of the

---

92 Weeks L (undated) *A Bridge of Voices.* Documentary audiotape, BBC Radio 4. Produced by Tom Morton for Sandprint Programs.
93 Williams D (1988) *Autism: An inside-out approach.* London: Jessica Kingsley (p137).
94 Higashida N (2013) *The Reason I Jump: The inner voice of a thirteen-year-old-boy with autism.* London: Sceptre.
95 Gray L (2013) *Vestibular System: Pathways and reflexes* [online]. Neuroscience online. Available at: http://neuroscience.uth.edu/s2/chapter11.html (accessed January 2014).
96 Goldberg JM, Wilson VJ, Cullen KE, Angelaki DE, Broussard DM, Buttner-Ennever J, Fukushima K & Minor LB (2012) *The Vestibular System: A sixth sense.* Oxford: Oxford University Press.

system they are affecting and how, if possible they can be compensated for. Further, scans reveal that Temple Grandin, who had considerable motor co-ordination problems, has a cerebellum that is 20% smaller than the average non-spectrum cerebellum[97]. (Looking back to shrinkage in the cerebellum of dancers who pirouette but who through rigorous training do not get dizzy (see p32), one might speculate as to whether this is due to Temple's evident self-discipline, retraining her brain to control her balance and movements.)

Many people on the spectrum devise their own methods of making up for the deficit in physical awareness of themselves in relation to their surroundings. For example, Damien Milton[98], who has Asperger's syndrome, tells us that he often walks on tiptoes in order to gain feedback of where he is in his environment. And Richard, who has severe autism and is hyposensitive to proprioception, also seeks pressure and walks on his toes. He responds by becoming attentive and thoughtful when strong pressure is applied to his feet. His body relaxes completely. Afterwards he goes out and sits in the garden quietly, trying out rubbing the soles of his feet on different surfaces (on a concrete block and on grass).

Judith Bluestone says:

'Because of faulty sensory integration, an individual with autism may perceive the world in such a radically different manner than others that from his perspective the behaviour makes sense. If a child has a severely under reactive vestibular system, he may frequently spin to attain the stimulation he needs ... or a child's vestibular system may be so under-stimulated that he tries to compensate for this lack through his visual system by spinning objects.'[99]

For example, Grandin spun coins and says that her total attention on this enabled her to cut out any other noises[100]. Judith Bluestone goes on to recommend a 'net swing' or 'dizzy disc' to meet the child's sensory needs.

The deficit in vestibular regulation has a number of different effects and, as Bluestone says, individuals tend to devise their own compensatory activities[101]. Temple Grandin famously designed a hydraulic machine based

---

97 Grandin T & Panek R (2013) *The Autistic Brain*. Boston, MA: Houghton, Mifflin and Harcourt.
98 Milton D (undated) *Nature's answer to over-conformity: Deconstructing pathological demand avoidance.* Unpublished essay.
99 Dejean V (2013) *Sensory Defensiveness in Children with Autism and PDD Dyspraxia* [online]. Available at: http://valeriedejean.org/uno7.html (accessed January 2014).
100 Webb T (1992) *A is for Autism*. London: BFI. (Film)
101 Bluestone J (2005) *The Fabric of Autism*. Bend, OR: The HANDLE Institute.

on a cattle press to calm herself and meet her need for pressure. A child who will not cross the road to his granny's house is perfectly able to do so when I suggest he is given two heavy shopping bags and directed to take them to her. Given a powerful physical stimulus, the message gets through, attention is refocused and he knows what he is doing.

The BioHug vest is a sophisticated approach to deep pressure application. Worn as a gilet, it has been developed in Haifa University to meet the needs of a child with sensory integration problems. Using compressed air, it delivers powerful pressure (that can be varied in order to avoid habituation so the brain does not get used to it and cease to pay attention) to the spine and lower neck areas – which is where people on the spectrum tell us that the pains they experience during the autonomic storm originate.

The mother of a child with severe autism describes the effect of using the BioHug vest with her son[102]:

'This vest was the first thing we have ever found that actually calmed Jon. We have had sensory assessments before and even our occupational therapists have not found any sensory equipment or activities that have helped in any way to calm him. So I was pretty amazed when it worked. Jon was quite resistant to the vest, but I think that's because it was too big and therefore heavy and a bit uncomfortable. I thought the motor noise would be an issue for him, but it wasn't at all. His activity level reduced significantly within a couple of minutes. He was able to concentrate on tasks while wearing the vest, such as playing the computer or watching TV. The most noticeable impact was in reducing aggression. He could go from very angry and aggressive to very calm in about 10 minutes.

'Normally when Jon really loses it, I would have to take him away to another room, use a solid hold and deep pressure for up to an hour to get him to an acceptable level. Meanwhile being punched and kicked half to death! Having a piece of equipment that did the same thing was unbelievable! We didn't quite get to the stage where Jon was able to recognise himself when he needed it, but that's partly age and partly because we only had it for a few months.

'In terms of the longer term benefits, the one thing we noticed was that as soon as the vest was off the effect was gone. So if we took it off too early you were back to square one. The activity level went right back up as soon as it was

---

102 Personal communication with author (undated).

turned off. This may reflect the level of Jon's problems. The sensory integration therapist we saw in London was of the opinion he was one of the most dysregulated children she had ever seen, so it could be that. And that would be typical of his responses to other sensory activities people have tried with him.

'Using the vest has had some other longer term benefits though. It has got Jon into the habit of agreeing to come for "calming down", which he used to be massively resistant to. I think because he saw the benefits he now realises it's a good thing. On the odd occasion he even tells me he needs it.'

At the opposite end of the autistic scale, Mike is very capable and able to tell us exactly what effect the vest had on his sensory overload. In addition to his visual distortions, he has more generalised sensory distortions. Here, he describes the 'before' and 'during' effects of wearing the vest:

'I got the BioHug vest tonight and have just got back from testing it out. I found it very securing, it greatly reduced my level of anxiety and took away a sensation that my body was aggressively trying to blow itself apart. Other major improvements included no urge to sway left or right in an open environment, no feeling of needing to walk faster than others and little or no disorientation. Considering this was the first time I tried it, I haven't been able to walk outside with no increased vital signs or low anxiety for two or three years.'

Later on:

'I've managed to walk to town today for the first time in about 10 or 11 months with only experiencing the onset of anxiety as soon as I walked out the door, but went away completely within three or four minutes. As I was feeling anxious at first, the BioHug responded as if it was just sucking up and stabilising the fear and anxiety flowing round my body, then releasing it like an exhaust pipe for toxic chemicals. In the afternoon I used it to go to Tesco, where I would usually suffer badly from spatial awareness and feel as if I'm being dragged towards the floor into a dark pit. Both of which I didn't experience at all.'

And again:

'When I was using it on Saturday, I could again get the feeling of comfortable pressurisation and security. However, when I tried to walk somewhere without it for a comparison, I could easily pickup on the feeling of depressurisation, and lightness (similar to a feather) and these effects combined create a sense of surliness, and the energy from that gets redirected to reinforce and worsen the disorientation. Like a greenhouse, it (the vest) is like the sun is the environment surrounding me, and glass panels is the section in my brain processing live sensory information. And usually the stronger the input (most commonly outdoors), the worse the heating effect gets. The BioHug vest is like a thermostat controller on a heating system (except for it functioning automatically in cases) where it can adjust the temperature in the greenhouse, causing a far more suitable and comfortable environment, enabling things in there to flourish.' (*sic*)

Six months later it appears that Mike is now no longer so dependent on the vest, suggesting that in some instances, persistent stimulation may be used to remediate damaged neural pathways. And Judith Bluestone's description of the 'tapping' handle treatment that she developed is also aimed at establishing connections which are under-performing or missing[103]. If one returns to the analogy of the goods yard, one might think of prioritising certain trains to run through scarce track.

Sensory integration

Prominent in the field of addressing vestibular/proprioception difficulties is Jane Ayres, who developed the approach known as Sensory Integration[104], which she defines briefly as, 'the organisation of sensory information for use. It is a neurological process that enables us to make sense of our world by receiving, modulating, organising and interpreting information that comes to our brain from our senses.'

Like a number of approaches which are developed marginally in relation to orthodox practice, Jane Ayre's Sensory Integration theory and conclusions remain controversial. Studies examining the effect of Sensory Integration treatment 'have found little support for the efficacy of SIT for treating children with various developmental disabilities'[105].

However, when it comes to autism, this conclusion may well depend on how the investigations were presented to the children, since many with severe

---

103 Bluestone J (2005) *The Fabric of Autism*. Bend, OR: The Handle Institute.
104 Ayres AJ (1972) *Sensory Integration and Learning Disorders*. Los Angeles, CA: Western Psychological Services.
105 Herbert JD, Sharp IR & Gaudiano BA (2002) Separating fact from fiction in the etiology and treatment of autism. *The Scientific Review of Mental Health Practice* **1** (1).

autism do not find it easy to co-operate with therapeutic approaches unless the therapist uses their personal body language as a 'way in'.

For example, Jane Horwood, a paediatric occupational therapist who specialises in using Sensory Integration, says that by using the specific body language of a child (Intensive Interaction – see **Appendix 2**), she was able to obtain co-operation in their first session as opposed to her normal expectation of the sixth session[106]. If the child fails to respond it is easy to assume that the interventions are not effective. Our studies have to provide and work through an environment that has meaning for the child. We need to circumvent their sensory triggers to distress by designing our interventions to work through the individual's personal sensory repertoire, so that our inputs are assessed by their brain as non-threatening and do not add to their stress levels.

In a recent review[107], Nancy Pollock points out that most people using Sensory Integration are occupational therapists and 'their approach reflects their aim to enhance the child's ability to participate in daily occupations'.

'Classical SI works through play with physically challenging objects such as physio balls, trampolines, rolls, and suspended equipment that provides intense proprioceptive, vestibular and tactile experiences.

'The alternative approach uses a Sensory Integration framework to help understand and explain children's behaviour, but rather than trying to remediate the underlying impairment, these methods are embedded in the child's daily routine and focus on adapting the children's environment. These approaches are designed to help children function to the best of their ability given their sensory processing capabilities as opposed to trying to change their underlying neurological function.'

In a comprehensive review[108], Case-Smith and Arbesman discuss the evidence basis for interventions adopted with individuals with autism and the case for use by occupational therapists. As with Sensory Integration Therapy, these approaches seem to fall into two categories: in a broad sense the therapist is either modifying the environment, or they are addressing neurological dysfunctions – repainting the walls or tinkering with the plumbing.

---

106 Horwood J (undated) Personal communication with author.
107 Pollock N (2009) Sensory Integration: A review of the current state of the evidence. *Occupational Therapy Now* **11** (5) 6–10.
108 Case-Smith J & Arbesman M (2008) Evidence-based review of interventions for autism used in or of relevance to occupational therapy. *The American Journal of Occupational Therapy* **62** (4) 416–429.

Promoting an autism faVourable environment (PAVE)

However, the children and adults we work with are not divided into neat compartments. Neurological developmental failures have behavioural consequences. As a 'last-port-of call' practitioner I am most often asked to see children and adults who have been unable to respond to a number of approaches. They may be extremely disturbed and sometimes aggressive but respond very quickly (sometimes within minutes) to interventions that address both their internal distortions and the external triggers that are overloading their weakened neurobiological systems.

In order to reach them, I need to produce an autism-friendly (autism faVourable) environment (PAVE)[109]. PAVE seeks to lower sensory distress by reducing the triggers to hyper and hypo sensitivities while at the same time increasing signals that do have meaning for the child, using powerful physical stimuli where appropriate and communicating through the child's own body language. Using the child's body language means not just working with what they are doing but, more importantly, how they are doing it, since this will reflect how they are feeling, giving insight into their affective state.

In sensory terms, Rico[110] is a child who shows vestibular disturbances and hypersensitivity to sound. He flinches when spoken to in his right ear. He cries and rocks on a chair in the corner of the classroom. He swings on curtains, giving himself vestibular stimulus. He hugs and scratches a cushion. He is sufficiently disturbed to be unable to join in classroom activities. I am able to get his attention by responding to his scratching sounds on a cushion of my own. He smiles and responds in turn.

Addressing his hypersensitivity to sound, I suggest that he is brought in a side door, avoiding the noisy school hall and put on a trampoline for 10 minutes – and subsequently for short intervals during the day. This gives him a vestibular stimulus that is sufficiently strong for him to focus on. When he gets off the trampoline, the 'jerk' (which Judith Bluestone describes as being so important in helping to close down her overloaded vestibular system) is sufficiently embedded in his neural pathways to last for some time (perseveration). However, as Wilbarger and Wilbarger point out, to be really effective, proprioceptive/vestibular interventions need

---

109 See Appendix 2.
110 Caldwell P (2012) *Delicious Conversations*. Brighton: Pavilion Publishing (p147).

topping up through the day, since the brain habituates and the effect fades eventually[111]. As the consequence of an intervention that addressed both his sensory and his communication needs, Rico is now able to engage with his class.

In this intervention, from never having met Rico previously, I have not only captured Rico's attention by responding to his body language, but have been paying him such intimate attention that it has also been possible to pick up his hypersensitivity to sound when he flinches and his vestibular problems when he is providing himself with a jerk by rocking and swinging: about an hour's work.

However, this is not a cure. All it has done is to provide an environment with which Rico can engage. It is dependent on maintenance – but he is now able to take part in the educational process from which his sensory difficulties had meant he was previously excluded.

Each child is completely different. In autism there are almost always a complex web of sensory problems and often interwoven psychological disturbances. Some will have a learning disability or sometimes a child will hold or beat its head where it hurts, but very often they will be unable to name their sensory needs and distortions even to themselves because they do not recognise them as anything other than the normal state of affairs.

For example, both Mike and Donna Williams express surprise at their new-found ability to process visual intake when given appropriate lenses. Observing the body language of a non-verbal man as he lifts his head when he puts on his new glasses: his eyes widen, jaw falls open as he swings his head round to gaze in astonishment at his newly found environment.

---

111 Wilbarger J & Wilbarger P (2008) *Sensory Defensiveness: A comprehensive treatment approach*. Troy, OH: Avanti Educational Programs.

Chapter six: Fight, freeze or flight

Survival

Autistic or not, we are born with a question mark hanging over our heads, an imperative that drives our very existence: in a hostile environment, will we or will we not survive? Even in the womb, from the moment of our conception, the struggle in which we are engaged is literally life against death. Are we furnished with a viable set of genes? Will we implant successfully? Is our uterine environment favourable? Are we strong enough to survive the one in eight possibility of being a twin? Can we survive the trauma of birth? As a neonate, can we bond with our mothers and they with us?

Leap frogging from then to now – looking around, I sense a world that is potentially hostile and by no means dedicated to my survival – but in a competing environment of around seven billion people, I have 'made it' more or less successfully. I am alive, fed, watered and housed, and apart from normal aging processes, basically undamaged. I have successfully paired off and raised a family. Blindfold I have walked through the minefield of chance and circumstance, and in biological terms I am a winner. All of which I take for granted.

So I am one of the lucky ones. My brain and body have been fine-tuned to recognise successfully those situations which are safe and those which are unfriendly or dangerous, and I have responded to these in such a way as to emerge reasonably unscathed. At least I have learned from them and shall be more aware in the future of when it is safe to tackle them head on or when I should withdraw.

Or shall I? It now emerges that exactly how I respond to challenging situations is complicated and not necessarily within my conscious grasp.

Against a background of autism, I want to draw together a number of themes that are currently emerging and address the astonishing systems that have evolved to promote survival and also some of the things that can go wrong if the system is badly wired up.

Temple Grandin[112] tells us, 'Fear is the main emotion in autism, like animals, looking for any little thing. Before I took anti-depressant drugs I was in a constant state of panic attacks all the time, looking for something that might be a threat … things scared me.'

We know that we need to feel safe. And yet it is evident that people with autism live on a knife edge. The brain is constantly informing their sympathetic nervous system that they are in danger, triggering responses that, at best, can appear to the non-autistic world as bizarre and sometimes hostile. But one of the puzzles of autism is the wide variety of these responses to stimuli that we who are not on the spectrum are unmoved by – but they may perceive as life-threatening. Under these circumstances of imminent catastrophe, why do children and adults on the spectrum respond to perceived threat in such different ways? Yes, they are different individuals and this is reflected in their behaviour – but there are broad bands of response which at first glance seem difficult to reconcile with each other.

Different responses to danger

Looking from the outsider's point of view, these are often summarised as, 'they are no trouble at all' (passive and withdrawn) to, 'they have 'challenging behaviour' (active and not easy to manage), neither of which description takes into account the sensory difficulties and distortions this particular person is struggling with and are at the root of their distress.

Why do some run away, some become immobile and some lash out? Can we draw together some of the disparate theories arising from theoretical points of view that focus on a particular set of responses such as, on the one hand, the autonomic storm[113] investigated by Ramachandran[114], and on the other, the catatonic reactions described by Lorna Wing,[115] both of which are encountered in clinical practice. Put simply, when they are upset, some people on the spectrum shut down their systems while others engage,

---

112 BBC (2006) The Woman Who Thinks Like a Cow. *Horizon.* BBC2. Archive film.
113 For descriptions of how it feels to be in the autonomic storm, see Appendix 3.
114 Ramachandran VS (2011) *The Tell-Tale Brain.* London: William Heinemann.
115 Wing L & Shaw A (2000) Catatonia in autism spectrum disorders. *British Journal of Psychiatry* **176** 357–362.

in the sense that they can become aggressive, quite different systems for separating oneself from the perceived source of their distress.

The amygdala

In autism, recent attention has been focusing on damage to the amygdala, a small almond-shaped organ in the brain. Always referred to in the singular, there are actually two, one on each side. It (they?) acts as our early warning system, detecting if an event presents as hostile[116], triggering evasive action in the case of perceived threat. Whether or not it is actually a real threat is irrelevant, it is the threshold at which the amygdala judges the level of danger to be hostile or potentially so that triggers the response known as the body's self-defence system, the 'fight-flight' response. More accurately, even if they may have a different aetiology, this is described as the fight-*freeze*-flight response: classically, if I see a snake, I might hit it, freeze or run. The question is which?

In all of us, messages from the sense organs are fast-tracked to the amygdala, which takes a snap decision as to whether or not what is happening represents a threat. At the same time, a slower message is on its way to the frontal cortex, where the event is 'put in context' and a decision made as to whether the immediate response was appropriate or needs to be adjusted. Where appropriate, a message is sent to the hypothalamus[117] (the brain's regulator) which:

1. activates the (ANS) autonomic nervous system[118], in particular the part of the nervous system that controls systems such as breathing rate, heart rate, sweating and digestion (the systems that 'work by themselves')

2. sets off the pituitary gland, which pumps hormones (releasing factors) into the bloodstream.

The body is now primed and ready for action through the fight, freeze, flight activity of the sympathetic nervous system, which increases the heart rate, stimulates the sweat glands, dilates the blood vessels in large muscles, dilates the pupils etc. At the same time, the parasympathetic system dampens down the digestive system. Skin colour changes with

---

116 Amaral DG & Corbett BA (2002) The amygdala, autism and anxiety. *Novartis Foundation Symposium* **2** 177–87.

117 Boeree CG (2009) *General Psychology: The emotional nervous system* (online). Available at: http://webspace.ship.edu/cgboer/limbicsystem.html (accessed December 2013).

118 The autonomic nervous system actually consists of two systems that work to balance each other to produce homeostasis (return to equilibrium): the **sympathetic system**, which in general activates the body, and the **parasympathetic system** that dampens down activity.

dilation or contraction of the capillaries. Usually, in addition to an increase in sweating, a child who is becoming distressed will flush, or in the case of a child who is black, his mother says he goes from ebony to matt black at the onset of what Ramachandran calls 'the autonomic maelstrom'[119]. (There are some children who show the opposite effect: their capillaries contract and colour drains.) Grandin spells out the relationship between cause and effect: when she hears a sudden noise she experiences a panic attack and her heart races[120].

Temple Grandin also tells us that scans have shown that her amygdala is enlarged, and comments that to know this helps her to keep her anxiety in check: 'even if the feeling of the threat is real, the threat is not.'[121]

While we have already looked at damage to the brain stem and cerebellum, it is becoming increasingly clear that damage in children with autism is not confined to one area of the brain but has multiple affects and there is wide variation within the spectrum. For example, Williams complains that putting a sensation in context is one of her great difficulties, so for her it is likely that this connection between the amygdala and cortex is not functioning effectively[122]. And Temple Grandin[123] talks about the difficulties that arise from failure of connectivity between different parts of the brain. She suggests we think of the brain:

'... as a big corporate office. Up at the top of the building you have the executive office. That's the frontal cortex. The frontal cortex has connections to all the different departments. The white matter is the brain's communication wires between the departments, analogous to telephone connections, email connections, internet connections. What happens in autism is those connections don't get connected, so it is difficult for them to talk to each other'.

In the same film, the psychologist Dougal Hare continues, 'Much of the behaviour of people with autism is an attempt to escape from situations they find distressing, to avoid sounds and lights that make them anxious and distressed.' I strongly agree – but should want to add that many are also on the run from labile emotional responses.

---

119 Ramachandran VS (2011) *The Tell-Tale Brain*. London: William Heinemann.
120 Grandin T (2013) *An Inside View of Autism* [online]. Autism Research Institute. Available at: http://www.autism.com/index.php/advocacy_grandin (accessed December 2013).
121 Grandin T & Panek R (2013) *The Autistic Brain*. Boston, MA: Houghton, Mifflin and Harcourt.
122 Williams D (1988) *Autism: An inside-out approach*. London: Jessica Kinsley Publishers.
123 Webb T (1992) *A is for Autism*. UK: BFI (Film).

Coping strategies: repetitive behaviour

People on the spectrum describe repetitive behaviour as a refuge from sensory anxiety and try to develop ways of managing their stress.

Some strategies focus attention by blocking out excess sensory stimuli and, incidentally, their source, losing contact with their environment (including people). In the absence of sensory tranquility and lacking intake that they can make sense of, people on the spectrum provide themselves with a point of focus to shut out the overload, so that there is at least *something* that is within their control. This comes in the form of self-stimulation ('stimming'), which provides meaningful stimulus that cuts down the level of stimuli to be processed, reducing the risk of entering the autonomic storm. In a world that is incoherent it helps to attend to at least one action that is predictable.

Listening to what people with autism are saying about their repetitive behaviours and what they are getting out of it, we get a picture of needing to protect themselves against overwhelming sensory input:

'I can focus intensely on cracking each and every knuckle on each hand, in a certain order. Over and over ... or counting tiles on the floor or panes in the windows etc. and the concentration and focus on the stim activity helps filter out the overwhelming stuff.'[124]

Temple Grandin says, 'I could sit on the beach and dribble sand for ages, each grain intrigued me as if I was a scientist looking at it through a microscope'[125]. On the other hand, Sian Barron says that when he does a repetitive behaviour, in a chaotic world, he knows what he is doing[126]. Naoki Hagashida[127] says about his repetitive behaviour, 'It doesn't come from our own free will. It's more like our brains keep sending out the same order, time and time again'. And O'Neill (who writes about herself in the third person) says, 'they focus upon some point of themselves to help calm them, especially when they feel threatened'. However, she also tells us

124 Online discussion board. *Could be Asperger some kind of lack of FILTERING?* Available at: www.wrongplanet.net/postt200620.html (accessed January 2014).
125 Webb T (1992) *A is for Autism*. UK: BFI (Film).
126 Barron S & Barron J (1992) *There's a Boy in Here*. New York: Simon and Schuster.
127 Higashida N (2013) *The Reason I Jump: The inner voice of a thirteen-year-old-boy with autism*. London: Sceptre.

that, 'routines and rituals bring comfort. They provide structure and safety and order'[128].

Such repetitive behaviours may be viewed by non-spectrum people as isolating and irritating, partly because to them they indicate that the person whose attention they may be trying to engage is focused elsewhere: interfering with even the possibility of communication. Efforts made to stop such repetitive activities raise the stress level and usually the behaviours become more pronounced – or the individual will slip into an alternative proactive way of doing something that makes sense to them.

However, when asked why people on the spectrum flap their hands, hum, cover their ears and rock, Carly, a young woman with severe autism who has learned to type fluently, simply replies, 'It's a way for us to drown out all the sensory input that overloads us all at once. We create output to block input'[129]. What they need most of all is a sensory environment that is predictable so they are not overwhelmed by (to them) nonsensical stimuli.

These individuals understand their repetitive behaviours in terms of trying to avoid getting sucked in to an autonomic storm. All the repetitive behaviours, the lining up cars, the scratching fingers, the flicking, flapping, the tearing paper, the endless reruns of a favoured video clip and the turning lights on and off are attempts by the brain to produce a sense of coherence in a world that for them is essentially chaotic in sensory terms.

For some, the search can become justified as an end in itself. Damien Milton describes his autistic son as having a dynamic connection to the sensory world, but he nevertheless continues that sometimes the sensory experience people on the spectrum live in is so chaotic that they 'seek out structure and routine to impose upon it, either derived internally or from outsiders'.

But to become totally immersed in sensory experience becomes a conversation held with oneself, and although embodiment of personal sensory experience is important, we need other people as well, not just for what they can give us but for what we can give them, so that we can enjoy the reciprocal flow of give and take. Donna warns us of the danger of such a monologue: 'in a relationship with yourself, the hypnotism, the grab, that pulls you back in there (to the inner world), is that when it's all turmoil out there, there's none of that in there, you just go.'

---

128 O'Neill JL (1999) *Through the Eyes of Aliens*. London: Jessica Kingsley.
129 See http://www.youtube.com/watch?v=vNZVV4Ciccg (accessed January 2014).

'...the wind can grow cold
in the depths of your soul, run and hide
to the corners of your mind
alone like a nobody nowhere.'[130]

So, while in sympathy with the retreat into an inner world of sensory self-stimulation as a means to avoid sensory overload, there is the danger of getting so sucked in that it becomes an end in itself, and in so doing losing the experience of affective companionship and intimacy. Donna says it's all right if you can visit it but if you have to live in it, it is a place of fear. Not a good place to be.

Looking at repetitive behaviour from the point of view of what is going on in the brain, post-mortem examinations of people on the spectrum show lesions in the amygdala[131]. Monkeys with damaged amygdala show motor stereotypies (for example, spinning) and have 'blank and expressionless faces'[132]. Quite how the lesions and the stereotypies are related, or if they are more in the nature of collateral damage, is not made clear. Nevertheless, looking at the functioning of the amygdala, in people with autism it would seem to be an unreliable instrument for predicting danger, seeing peril where there is no actual threat. At least this is what it looks like to the outsider – but this overlooks the omnipresent threat posed by hypersensitivities to sensory input, of triggering the body's self-defence system and so tipping the brain and body into an autonomic storm with its confusing and painful consequences.

Hirstein *et al*[133] make a distinction between two types of reactivity in children on the spectrum.

Type A has a very high level of sympathetic activity (which can be shut off by repetitive activities such as playing with dried beans). Type A people on the spectrum say about their self-stimuli:

1. 'When I do this I know what I am doing.'[134]

2. 'When I spun the coin I could cut out all the other sounds.'[135]

130 Williams D (1992) *Nobody Nowhere: The remarkable autobiography of an autistic girl*. London: Jessica Kingsley.
131 Bauman ML & Kemper TL (1994) Neuroanatomic observations of the brain in autism. *The Neurobiology of Autism*. Baltimore, MD: John Hopkins University Press.
132 Bachevalier J (1996) Brief report: medial temporal lobe and autism: a putative model in primates. *Journal of Autism and Developmental Disorders* **26** (2) 217–220.
133 Hirstein W, Iverson P & Ramachandram VS (2001) Autonomic responses of children to people and objects. *Proceedings of the Royal Society of London, Series B: Biological Sciences* **268** (1479).
134 Barron S & Barron J (1992) *There's a Boy in Here*. New York: Simon and Schuster.
135 Webb T (1992) *A is for Autism*. UK: BFI (Film).

Type B children have a very low level of SCR (Skin Conductance Responses – a measure of autonomic activity), one that relates only to behaviour such as extreme self-injury. Hirstein suggests that, whereas the high SCR child will engage in damping down activities to reduce autonomic activity, the low SCR child is 'engaging in self-injurious behaviour or risk-taking in order to produce more autonomic activity'.

Hirstein goes on to suggest that the limbic autonomic network attaches value to concepts developed in the higher cortical centres, so that such choices that are made promote survival. This could be vital in learning that other people are valuable and if it is not working the child will not learn to relate to other people. He goes on to say, 'the children need to engage… in relaxing activities when their arousal levels get too high'.

In this context, I want to consider working with a typical Type A child, Ricky. In the playground it is clear that he is unhappy and he either hides in a corner or runs around in a distressed state, flapping his hands or biting them. This is the world of sensory chaos and, as Hirstein says, he seeks an activity he can focus on so that he can cut down his high arousal levels. Given the opportunity, Ricky will play endlessly with dried corn, dribbling it through his fingers into a box making a rattling sound – for hours if left to do so. He does not like being interrupted. However, what I do notice is that when he is not feeling the corn, he is rubbing his fingers together, so the corn rubbing is giving him a stronger proprioceptive version of the stimulus than he can give himself without it. It is the physical sensation located on his fingertips he is after, the stronger the better. His sensory overload is reduced as he focuses on this powerful proprioceptive stimulus. But, in order to maintain this state of sensory calm, he has to give his total attention to his finger stimulation – and in so doing, he cuts off from his surroundings and from other people. As Hirstein suggests, he is using repetitive behaviour to dampen his autonomic over-activity.

Hirstein suggests that both A and B type children are looking for homeostasis, a relatively stable and level playing field, holding the balance between ability to function and sensory distress.

Self-injury

Some people on the spectrum offer alternative views as to why they are self-injuring. Lindsey Weekes[136] says he would bang his head on the wall or run in front of a car, anything to stop the pain he experiences. Judith Bluestone is more specific when she tells us that banging her head shuts down her overloaded auditory/balance system.

The most powerful description of self-injury, however, comes from Donna Williams[137]:

'Self-abuse was the outward sign of an earthquake nobody saw. I was like an appliance during a power surge. As I blew fuses my hands pulled out my hair and slapped my face. My teeth bit my flesh like an animal bites the bars of its cage, not realising the cage was my own body. My legs ran round in manic circles, as though they could outrun the body they were attached to. My head hit whatever was next to it, like someone trying to crack open a nut that had grown too large for its shell. There was an overwhelming feeling of inner deafness – deafness to self that would consume all that was left in a fever pitch of silent screaming.'

Over time it appears that the amygdala may become more skilled at assessing the level of danger that a potential threat poses and create a 'salience landscape', detailing the emotional significance of the individual's environment[138]. Sapolsky[139] has shown that in response to rapid stimulation, the synapses become hyper-responsive, subsequently responding to a lower level of stimulation so the threshold for triggering the self-defence system is reduced as the messages get hard-wired in. Ramachandran[140] sums this up by suggesting that, in individuals with autism, the salience landscape is distorted, events seeming to be dangerous that in reality present no threat.

Emotional overload

So far we have focused on sensory overload triggered by external stimuli,

---

136 Weekes L (undated) *A Bridge of Voices.* Documentary audiotape, BBC Radio 4. Produced by Tom Morton for Sandprint Programs.
137 Williams D (1994) *Somebody Somewhere: Breaking free from the world of autism.* London: Jessica Kingsley.
138 Ramachandran VS & Oberman LM (2006) *Broken Mirrors: A Theory of Autism* [online]. Scientific American. Available at: http://cbc.ucsd.edu/pdf/brokenmirrors_asd.pdf (accessed January 2014).
139 Sapolski RM (2005) *Biology and Human Behaviour: The neurobiological origins of individuality* (2nd edition). Chantilly, VA: The Teaching Company.
140 Ramachandran VS (2011) *The Tell-Tale Brain.* London: Random House.

such as too much bright light or overlapping sound, that come directly from the environment. But for some people on the spectrum, it is their disturbed affective state that triggers sensory overload rather than a direct response to an external event. This is more of a secondary internal hypersensitivity: an unregulated emotional response to a perceived event, one that might strike the non-autistic observer as neutral or mildly irritating rather than (sometimes devastatingly) sad.

Responses are so different. While Michelle Dawson[141] (herself autistic) says that she does not attach an emotional response to concrete objects, a friend on the autistic spectrum tells me that she became distraught at the sight of a broken deck-chair. This might seem a wildly 'over-the-top' reaction to a non-spectrum person but it reflects the overreaction of a labile autonomic nervous system which floods her with distress. And this is real, not vicarious emotion. She was swept by a tidal wave of feeling that left her weeping.

In describing this as emotional overload, Donna Williams says it is sometimes so powerful that it feels as if the individual is being attacked, triggering the body's self-defence system, so they may respond with aggression to protect themselves.

'Unprocessed, indistinguishable sensations of pure unprocessed contextless emotions (that were probably connected to information that was not yet fully processed) too often would suddenly flood me in a heap after their immediate context had gone, leaving me sensorily and/or emotionally overloaded to painful extremes. These felt like fits or attacks...'[142]

Surprisingly, negative reactions may come as a shock to a well-intentioned non-spectrum person offering emotional warmth. The effect on her mother is described by Temple Grandin[143]. Her mother wrote, 'If Temple does not want me, I'll keep my distance,' to which Temple responds, 'It was not that she did not want her but that the sensory overload of a hug shorted out her nervous system'.

We do not expect those we are engaged with to respond to our positive overtures with hostility, so emotional overload is often overlooked as a trigger or just written off as an inexplicable outburst. Where it occurs, it

---

141 Dawson Michelle. Autism researcher at Riviere-de-Prairies hospital, University of Montreal – quoted by Temple Grandin, no reference given.
142 Williams D (1988) *Autism: An inside-out approach*. London: Jessica Kingsley (p91).
143 Grandin T & Panek R (2013) *The Autistic Brain*. Boston, MA: Houghton, Mifflin and Harcourt (p8).

is a problem for teachers who use praise to encourage their students to learn. It is hard for those of us not on the spectrum to understand why our friendly overtures are being rejected. It is also difficult to know how to respond, since a response that is wiped of emotion feels to us cold and counterintuitive. It feels unnatural for us to deliberately avoid eye contact or speak to someone indirectly in the third person. But where a non-spectrum person might feel embarrassment, an individual with autism can be totally overwhelmed. It can be a smile, or any form of emotional warmth that sets off sensory overload or an autonomic storm.

Sometimes the trigger to emotional overload is even more puzzling, such as a sensitivity to names, which, although we may not think about them in this way, seem to carry an emotional tag. One form of childhood teasing is to play around with someone's name in a mocking way to the point where they feel belittled. Somehow, one's name reflects one's personhood and although we will pretend we do not care, we feel exposed if it is tampered with. On the other hand, we use affectionate diminutives to bond with those we feel close to. But it is the feeling of exposure (good or bad) that is so embedded in some individuals on the autistic spectrum – and multiplied far beyond what the non-spectrum individual might experience.

For example, a 16 year old has a surge of painful emotion when he hears his name – but he is able to respond when I suggest that we email each other using our initials instead of our names. Somehow we have managed to work round the link to affect.

Donna Williams provides us with insight into what it actually feels like to experience emotional overload in her remarkable book, *Autism – An Inside Out Approach*[144]. Published around 25 years ago, this book still offers the most profound exploration of what it is like to experience the inner world of autism, where, because of her sensory problems, she was forced to live in a world that was too much for her to cope with: 'one that she could not only not understand but also could not stand it.'[145]

Reading it, we are struck again with the realisation that we really are looking at a different world, where the sensations that we commonly perceive are experienced in a completely different way, one where 'meaning and significance rarely connect with the context that provokes them … so that they may be impossible to comprehend… The effect on the body may be

---

144 Williams D (1988) *Autism: An inside-out approach*. London: Jessica Kingsley (p215).
145 *Ibid* (p1).

so extreme that it may feel that it is too difficult for the body to sustain…
it may result in severe tremors, palpitations and hyperventilation.'

These signals to the body are interpreted as 'danger' or 'an attack on the
body that needs to be defended against as a matter of survival'. Such
emotional hypersensitivity can push a person beyond the limits of their
emotional tolerance to systems dissociation, or systems can shut down
completely, and/or result in painful sensory hypersensitivities. If the
sensory overload is not diffused, shutdown means there will be a temporary
inability to process touch, sound and visual information for meaning, and
also to access communication with movement or speech.

Donna says that some people are so emotionally hypersensitive that they
cannot stand the feeling of self-exposure when someone demonstrates
an interest. Their affective response is 'triggered much too easily, so that
conscious awareness [of self] is experienced as painful'. 'The result of
exposure anxiety,' Williams writes, 'is an intense rawness that is easily
mistaken for pain.'

If I have borrowed heavily from Donna's account it is because of her
extraordinary capacity to reflect on her emotional landscape, in a way
that few others who are so deeply embedded in the autistic spectrum have
found possible.

Layer on layer. Before leaving the neurological confusion and pain triggered
by external stimuli and the internal stimuli of emotional overload, we
should not overlook the additional psychological distresses that can be set
off by trauma.

This was particularly brought home to me when I was asked to work with
Rachel, a middle-aged woman who has spent a little less than 40 years of
her life in a long-stay institution. She is now living in a caring residential
house. Although like a number of people labelled as learning disabled who
have spent long periods in what were known as mental handicap hospitals,
she does not have a formal diagnosis of autism, this possibility is suggested
by the way that she retreats into her own world using compulsive repetitive
behaviour; collecting cards and storing wads of them in her bag and taking
them out and licking them. Further acquaintance suggests that the physical
feedback she is giving herself is orally based – not only does she feel the
embossed numbers with her tongue but she also plays with her tongue and
grinds her teeth. Focusing on this, she is having a conversation with herself

that probably stems from the time when she lived in an environment that made no sense to her and she almost certainly experienced as threatening. Autistic or not, she has retreated into her own inner world.

Rachel has a specific behaviour that is difficult to manage. When someone leaves the house, she goes and stands by the door looking out of the glass panel. She screams and stamps, becoming deeply distressed. It is known that this behaviour predates her coming out of hospital and many remedial attempts such as diversion have been tried without success. (Trying to let her know they will return has not been effective.) I am told that these episodes can last for up to two hours. Even when she comes away from the door she will look out of the window, and sometimes returns to the door and starts again. Possible triggers that have been suggested are that she feels she is 'missing out', or that she wants to leave the house – but the depths of her despair suggest that there may be an even more fundamental explanation and I begin to suspect that she is re-enacting the trauma of abandonment she experienced as a child when she was first left in hospital.

Working from this assumption, I first show Rachel's manager how to use her body language to build up a non-verbal conversation with her. She responds very quickly when we use the rhythm of her 'teeth grinding' by stroking a pencil over the ridged network of the fan cover, nodding our heads in time to hers, sighing, sticking out our tongues in response to hers and generally tuning in to her sounds and movements. Rachel smiles and laughs and claps her hands. She becomes attentive and responsive and her obsessive card licking is reduced.

We set it up so that by the time her fellow residents leave the house, Rachel is relaxed and enjoying interaction. When she hears they are leaving and the door shuts, she gets up and goes to the door as usual and presses her face against the panel of glass. I get her manager to stand beside her (close enough for Rachel to feel the pressure of her body) and continue to respond to her sighs and sounds and movements, tuning in to how she is expressing how she feels by rubbing her back in time to these, physically acknowledging her grief. Her manager keeps her hand on Rachel's back for reassurance. Although her breathing rate goes up (an indication of the sympathetic nervous system's rising stress level) and she heaves a bit, she does not cry or show the deep distress that normally accompanies the departure of the other residents. After a short while she returns to the sitting room and looks out of the window. Her breathing rate calms quite quickly. At no time does she become distraught.

What we did with Rachel was quite physical and needs to be thought of in the context of the level of her distress. Why was she getting so distraught? What we were trying to deliver was a combination of pre-emptive diversion enabling her to relax, and contingent comforting to reassure her. Rachel needs physical containment to remind her that she is safe and that the people who support her care for her.

Chapter seven: Friends, lions and tortoises

Porges' theory

To get a better understanding of which way we (non-spectrum as well as those on with autism) will react to stress and perceived danger, we need to look at the Polyvagal Theory[146], which relates neurophysiology and neuroanatomy to behavioural responses.

If we think about toads and snakes, and even crocodiles, they sit around a lot and don't use a great deal of energy. As Else and Hulbert put it: 'reptiles (and amphibians) get around with a reliable but underpowered engine whereas mammals locomote with a supercharged engine that can function for only short periods before needing to refuel.'[147]

Professor Porges points out that the human brain has evolved by incorporating structures and systems inherited from these, our evolutionary ancestors. They are still operative and under certain circumstances we will favour the more primitive option over our more advanced systems.

At the centre of our defence system is the vagal nerve complex, which Porges describes as a 'conduit' with efferent nerves from the brain to organs such as the heart, lungs and gastric organs (motor nerves telling them what to do), and afferent nerves from these organs to the brain (sensory nerves), informing the brain of the state of the organ.

---

146 Porges SW (2011) *The Polyvagal Theory: Neurophysiological foundations of emotions, attachment, communication and self-regulation*. New York: W.W. Norton and Company.
147 Else PL & Hulbert AJ (1981) Comparison of the 'mammal machine' and the 'reptile machine': energy production. *American Journal of Physiology* **240 (1)** 1208–1210.

The vagal system

This vagal system is divided into the (older) dorsal branch, which serves the low energy requirement system of reptiles and amphibians, and the more evolved and sophisticated system, which meets the higher energy requirements of mammals, including humans.

Nevertheless, in spite of having a simple vagal system with unmyelinated (unsheathed) nerves, reptiles have managed to develop a remarkable range of self-defence systems. First of all there is camouflage in the hope that the predator will overlook the presence of its prey and which requires no activity at all. Once spotted, the tortoise retreats into his shell. Given the opportunity, most snakes and lizards will make a run for it and turtles and crocodiles will dive into water and sink out of sight, the exception being the snapping turtle, which is an early example of a 'fight' response, extending its neck and biting. A rather more drastic response is that of some geckos, skinks and lizards who shed their tails, which remain wriggling to attract attention while the animal itself runs away. Some snakes will hiss and expand their necks to make themselves look larger and the rattlesnake rattles its tail to ward off perceived threat. However, quite a number of snakes will feign death. The most striking example is the hog-nosed snake, which goes through a very convincing sequence of thrashing around in a death agony, flipping over on to its back, lying belly up, mouth open and tongue hanging out in floppy immobilisation. At the same time it oozes a foul secretion smelling of decay. Predators lose interest because they do not care to eat carrion.

Higher up the evolutionary tree, some birds show trance-like behaviour when afraid. Opossums 'play possum', while at the same time secreting a smell of rotting corpses from the anus. However, if the death-feigning strategy is invoked in mammals it may have unexpectedly negative results, the outcome being physiologically damaging – slowing down breathing rate or heart rate to dangerous levels, accidentally so to speak, causing their own death[148]. Critically, this level of response to stress (reversion to the more primitive reptilian strategy) is characterised by low level muscular tone, the defensive state being immobilised and floppy.

With their higher metabolic requirements, mammals have developed a more effective sympathetic nervous system that mobilises the body's systems

---

148 Our muscles are not normally completely relaxed, so muscular tone is defined as the continuous and partial contraction state of the muscles, or its resistance to passive stretch during resting state.

into action, so that it now has a choice and is capable of flight or fight, as discussed in the previous chapter. Under the influence of the sympathetic nervous system we run away or feel surges of anger. I once heard Temple Grandin talk about the lion raging in her head. In contrast to the 'reptilian' response to danger, this type of response is associated with raised pulse rate and increased muscle tone.

However, such a system is expensive in terms of energy, so humans have evolved and perfected an even more sophisticated alternative: the possibility of avoiding dangerous situations in the first place by deliberately setting up systems that promote safety. This has been achieved by the development of a complex myelinated parasympathetic vagal system. (As opposed to the unsheathed nerves of the reptilian system, myelinated nerves are surrounded by a sheath of proteins and phospholipids that enable it to conduct neural impulses faster.) In addition to powering bodily organs and acting as a brake on the heart, the vagal system now involves innervations of facial muscles giving rise to emotional expression. In addition to showing others how we feel, this facial expression allows humans to interpret the intentions and feelings of others and to signal our own, so that we become part of a socially bonded defensive network. Being friends and belonging to a group are a pre-emptive system that avoids having to expend a lot of valuable energy on defence: prevention is better than cure.

So in humans, the activity of the sympathetic system is balanced by the action of the parasympathetic vagal system. In theory at least, we are primed to communicate rather than fight – at least we now have this possibility, even if we do not always exercise it.

Self-defence

According to Porges' theory, if social engagement is insufficient to protect us, the brain/body may resort to the less sophisticated system. The body's self-defence system kicks in and we prepare to fight or run: under even more extreme conditions, we may revert to immobilisation and pass out. The effect of this is to cut off communication with the world outside, total retreat into an inner world, isolated, unresponsive and immobile. In the choice between parasympathetic or sympathetic response, Porges suggests that the choice is involuntary and which system is dominant varies from individual to individual. He cites the example of a plane diving in distress (which subsequently landed safely). Some passengers reacted to fear by screaming but one woman reverted to the primitive immobilisation system and feinted, passing out completely and in the affective sense, feeling nothing[149].

In applying Porges' theory to autism, the literature and terminology become somewhat confused between what is variously described as 'immobilisation', 'catatonia' and 'catatonia-like states', 'freeze' and 'shut-down'. Looking at the literature, it is clearly describing a spectrum of reactions and partial reactions rather than a single response. While suggesting that, in evolutionary terms, the behaviours probably derive from the need to escape from predators, in a paper titled *Scared Stiff*, Moskowitz[150] makes the distinction between 'Unresponsive Immobility' or 'Tonic Immobility' (TI) and 'Attentive Immobility'. TI is described as a fear strategy, characterised by lack of response to stimuli and lack of movement – often in an unusual posture that can last for seconds to hours. Muscles are rigid, so this is a high tone response – not at all the same as the immobilisation-floppy behaviour so clearly demonstrated in a photograph of a very long python sagging between the hands of its row of seven captors who picked it up under the illusion that it was dead. When they put it down it slithered away[151].

An alternative response to fear under the control of the parasympathetic nervous system anecdotally reported in adolescents with intellectual disability and autism, is relaxation of the sphincter muscle, so they urinate or defecate.

In contrast, Attentive Immobility is a transient delay, while deciding on the best escape strategy. This is the type of freeze reaction that might result when a bomb goes off and everyone hits the floor while they assess the severity of the threat and decide on the best options for escape.

Neither TI nor Attentive Immobility really address the multiplicity of shutdown reactions found in autism. The confusion possibly arises from trying to combine disparate behaviours that present as similar but have different aetiologies, or come from the same place but present differently along this spectrum of options. In this context, the brain may shut down one of the senses in order to have the capacity to process another. Naoki Higashida[152] says he does not look at people when they are talking because

---

149 Porges S & Buczynski R (undated) *Polyvagal Theory: Why this changes everything* [online]. Mansfield, CT: National Institute for the Clinical Application of Behavioural Medicine. Available at: www.nicabm. com (accessed January 2014).

150 Moskowitz AK (2004) Scared stiff: catatonia as an evolutionary-based fear response. *Psychological Review* **111** (4) 984–1002.

151 Personal communication with author (undated).

152 Higashida N (2013) *The Reason I Jump: The inner voice of a thirteen-year-old-boy with autism*. London: Sceptre.

he is trying to listen to the other person with all his senses. 'When we're fully focused on working out what the heck it is you're saying, our sense of sight sort of zones out.' Grandin[153] makes the point that, as a child (with auditory processing problems who was sensorily overloaded by too much speech, which she could not process), she might either shut down sensory intake to block feelings, or throw a tantrum. One child – alternative responses.

Autistic immobilisation

Starting with limp immobility, Loos Miller and Loos[154] use the term 'shutdown' to describe a sequence of behaviour in an autistic child who, 'when under pressure to perform tasks that she found difficult became disorientated, unresponsive, sleepy, immobile and limp to the touch and then fell asleep for up to two hours'. Even when offered a reward she wanted, her pencil would fall from her hand, and saying, 'I have to sleep,' she was unable to complete the task. It was not possible to arouse her by touch.

As a practitioner, I am asked to see very few children who are reacting to stress in this way (probably because they do not present the same challenges as a child who hits people or is hurting themselves). However, in Nicole (who we met on p.23), her hypotonia (floppiness) is probably related to the complex genetic phenotype of Down's syndrome[155]. In the context of her hypotonia, it may be her only option in response to fear, since she does not have the experience of being able to recruit the alternative of immediately active high-tone musculature.

Nicole was diagnosed as having hypotonia as an infant and was unable to walk until she was five. Since she has problems with the presence of too many people and with direct speech, she finds school extremely sensorily stressful and simply sits in a chair and goes to sleep. Seeing her distress, her mother decides to home-school her. Since she told her she need not go any more – and demonstrated this by getting her to help put her school uniform in the bin – Nicole is happier, less stressed, more responsive and

---

153 Grandin T & Panek R (2013) *The Autistic Brain*. Boston, MA: Houghton, Mifflin and Harcourt.

154 Loos Miller IM & Loos HG (2004) *Shutdowns States and Stress Instability in Autism* [online]. Available at: http://www.de-poort.be/cgi-bin/Document.pl?id=374 (accessed January 2014).

155 The complex phenotype that constitutes Down's syndrome may in large part simply result from the over-dosage of only one or a few genes within the DCR and/or region D21S55-MX1. See Delabar JM, Theophile D, Rahmani Z, Chettouh Z, Blouin JL, Prieur M, Noel B & Sinet PM (1993) Molecular mapping of twenty-four features of Down syndrome on chromosome 21. *European Journal of Human Genetics* 1 (2) 114–24.

has become able to allow activities she could not physically tolerate before, such as having her toenails cut.

On the other hand, Alex is truly stiff and has been from the age of 19. Only his father can persuade him to bend. As a child he was very passive, never retaliating at school if he was being bullied. This is in agreement with Wing and Shah who suggest that individuals who are passive in their social interactions are particularly vulnerable to severe exacerbations of catatonic features[156].

So, in people on the autistic spectrum, immobilisation can be associated both with high muscle tone, freezing as in 'posturing' (when the body gets stuck in a particular position being unable to carry through a sequence of movements), or low muscle tone, as when Nicole retreats into sleep. Confusingly, Donna Williams describes herself as having both active behaviours and floppy, what she calls body-disconnected, behaviours[157]. Lift her arm up and release it and it falls like a stone.

She tells us that around the age nine to 11, she had had a breakthrough interpreting language – but while this led to an increase in understanding, it also resulted in an overload of affective pressure. At first she first shook her head and her hands so vigorously that it was as if she was trying to flap the latter off her wrists like a rag doll. Following this, she says:

'I had a sort of emotional breakdown and my body went rigid and I was miles away from my body and mind. I went through a regression for some months, ended up out of school, got sent up to the countryside to recover and returned in a daze, progressively getting my body and mind back by the age of 14 a few schools later. I couldn't associate this physical rigidity with the rag doll aspect but understanding that someone with poor muscle tone (hypotonia) can also go through an episode of catatonia brought on by a severe untreated mood and anxiety disorder, helps me understand the interactions of the two.'

Apart from total body shutdown states, with either high or low muscle tone, although they arise out of the need to protect themselves from sensory overload and the autonomic storm, most shutdowns in autism are

---

156 Wing L & Shah A (2000) Catatonia in autistic spectrum disorders. *British Journal of Psychiatry* **176** 357–362.

157 Williams D (2009) *Hypotonia and the Presumption of Mental Retardation* [online]. Edmonton, AB: Austism at home series. Available at: http://www.autismathomeseries.com/library/2009/08/hypotonia-and-the-presumption-of-mental-retardation (accessed January 2014).

partial: when the processing system is in danger of being overloaded the brain simply cuts down on further activity in one mode or another. The body remains alert and muscle tone is high. Sometimes the individual can be seen to be trying to 'organise the next step'. When one system or the other stops working, Donna Williams calls it, 'going into mono' or 'Systems Shutdown', as in periods when she could either see or feel, but not both at the same time[158]. As she uses it, Systems Shutdown is a comprehensive term which includes inhibition of either cognition or mobilisation functions. This seems to equate with Wing and Shah's definition of catatonia: 'increased slowness affecting movement and speech' and 'difficulty in initiating and completing actions', to 'freezing in postures' – all under the umbrella term of 'catatonia'[159].

During this suspended time, both children and adults on the spectrum may be completely still and not be able to move on at all, even while they are obviously trying to do so. But in spite of immobilisation, muscular tone remains high. In some cases they are responsive, in others they retreat into their own world. What they appear to have in common is a blockage preventing an action sequence: they know they want to do but, because of a faulty processing system, need time and space to work out how to do it.

Such people on the spectrum may physically come to a halt, sometimes in strange postures. A man stops with his leg in the air as he tries to walk through a door. He is standing upright (with high muscular tone) but is immobilised[160]. A child comes to a halt on the way from her classroom to the hall. She cannot move on. Another child cannot cross the road. A woman looks at the ceiling and gets locked into uncontrollable and prolonged spasms of crying or laughter that does not appear related to circumstances. Yet another becomes unable to break out of a particular phrase, which she will repeat for hours.

Some light is shed on these apparent paralyses by a man who comes to a stop while turning over a page. When asked why he cannot continue he says he 'needs time to think'[161]. That is, he needs some time to organise the necessary motor pattern of movements. A friend on the spectrum tells me she deliberately shuts down on emotional hypersensitivity as it is so stressful, which implies that in her case it is now under her conscious

---

158 Williams D (1988) *Autism: An inside-out approach*. London: Jessica Kingsley (p121).
159 Wing L & Shah A (2000) Catatonia in autistic spectrum disorders. *British Journal of Psychiatry* **176** 357–362.
160 Elspeth Bradley (undated) Personal communication with autism.
161 *Ibid.*

control. I suspect that at first it was an unconscious response, one that she eventually realised was helpful and adopted it as a strategy that helped her to avoid sensory overload.

From the point of view of the practitioner, it may be very much more difficult to make contact with someone in these suspended states than with those who have opted for a more active defence – at least where there is aggression or flight, the individual has not always turned off their receptive processing, and therefore their ability to connect, so there is the possibility that they may perceive one's overtures.

On the other hand, in one variety or another, many of them appear to experience the suspension of their ability to complete an action that Pranve so clearly demonstrates (see p77).

Systems shutdown

Looking at the tendency of people with autism to 'get stuck', either in the middle of a behaviour or in its initiation, Donna Williams has a lot to say about systems shut-down, which she relates to sensory overload and attempts by her brain to focus on one system only, in order to reduce her sensory intake and consequent confusion[162].

Under these circumstances, her brain makes an unconscious choice to shut down one sensory channel such as vision in order to focus on listening. She says this may actually speed up total processing, rather than the brain getting totally overwhelmed by an otherwise confusing jumble. (This again points towards a processing bottleneck, possibly in the Purkinje cells where it is suggested that visual and auditory signals may be competing for reduced capacity (see Chapter 2).) She points out that under such conditions it is a mistake to force someone to look while they are listening, since the additional stimuli increase the amount of processing necessary[163].

This shutdown of functions may result in an inability to access either movement or speech effectively. It can also occur as a result of emotional hypersensitivity 'so that one becomes disconnected with even intense thoughts and feelings intensely present before shutdown'. Donna Williams calls this a 'mental stutter'[164].

---

162 Williams D (1988) *Autism: An inside-out approach*. London: Jessica Kingsley.
163 *Ibid*
164 *Ibid*

Apart from involuntary utterances, our brains have to know, either consciously or unconsciously, what they are trying to say. We need a plan. But a plan is not enough. Before we can speak, our brain has to mobilise the very complex sequences of muscular movements in the right order in order to fulfil the plan. This is particularly true of speech.

Near the end of a three-hour intervention, in film of an unpublished intervention now used for training, it is evident that Pranve (who is non-verbal except for the phrase, 'Where's Charlene?') is trying to sing a nursery rhyme. We see and hear him humming several times an approximation of the pitch and rhythm of the first line and then very softly putting the words in. Having done this, he struggles with the second line. Again, the rhythm comes first, if a bit unsteadily, and then he places his head in all sorts of positions so that one can clearly see actualised the phrase, 'getting one's head round things'. His jaw wobbles. He rests for a minute or so and finally comes out strongly with the first two lines of 'Baa-Baa Black Sheep', something his mother and speech therapist who are present assure me that he has never done before. Wherever he has got it from, the lead-in to his performance makes it is absolutely clear that Pranve knows exactly what he wants to do but there is a delay in his being able to mobilise the sequence of muscle motor movements necessary to sing his song. He needs time (and practice shots) to sort these out. Is this what the man who cannot complete turning the page means when he says he needs time to think?

The practitioner's instinct is to use cues and prompts to help re-engage attention and move the action along. The problem with this approach is that it may add to the sensory overload, particularly if speech or similar cognitive processes are used. Sensory approaches are more likely to be successful. Take for example the child who cannot move from her class to the hall who is given a chair to carry which she will sit on when she gets there, or the child who cannot cross the road but manages to do so successfully when he is given heavy shopping bags to carry. In each case it is the powerful proprioceptive stimulus (but one that is part of the activity) that re-engages the brain and sets it on its way. The woman who looks at the ceiling and is locked into endless crying is able to stop when I offer her a cup of coffee – which she loves – but seeing it is not enough; it is not until I hold it close enough to her nose for the smell to get carried up on the steam that she responds.

On the other hand, following a traumatising incident, Des became severely catatonic and locked into a posture that looked extremely uncomfortable, lying on his bed with his unsupported shoulders and head upright. However when his bedside lamp was knocked over and broken he briefly becomes unlocked in order to help his father mend it. It is clear that he is interested in how it fits together and this mechanical interest temporarily overrides his fixed position. This offers a possible pathway to be developed to help Des regain his trust and reconnection with the world round him.

Systems shutdown, or disconnectedness from the body, can get in the way of using body language to communicate, since it is not possible to communicate with others if one does not have a physical connection with one's self. Jamie, who is non-verbal, patrols the classroom endlessly, tapping himself with a skittle and living in his own world[165]. He does not engage through my response to his sounds. Seeing that he is giving himself proprioceptive stimuli by pacing and hitting himself, I decide to enhance the input he is giving himself by using a toy turtle that vibrates. This gives him a powerful input that reconnects him with his body. He now knows where he is and notices others as separate – he spots the camera men at this stage and waves to them. He begins to use his sounds in answer to mine, copying mine, rather than as random utterances. He discovers how to switch the vibration unit on and off, so I link this action with his sounds, giving a surprised 'Ooh' every time he throws the switch. His pacing stops and he comes and sits near me. His eye contact improves. He is interested in me now and keeps referring back to see what my response will be to the increasingly varied initiatives that he is making. He copies my hand movements and pushes my hand up, verbalising 'Up' as he does it. He smiles and laughs, hiding his face in his hands shyly with pleasure. He has come a long way over the bridge of proprioception from his lost inner world.

Many questions remain, however. For example, is catatonia primarily a fear response as Porges suggests or, as Moskowitz acknowledges in an article that otherwise mainly supports Porges' view, the contrary position? 'It is certainly conceivable,' he argues, 'that [it is] abnormalities in the motor loop that, in and of themselves, could cause catatonic symptoms.'[166] Motor disorders (as would seem more likely in the shutdown behaviours of autism), or panic?

I should like to suggest the possibility that it may be both, that it is fear and anxiety of sensory overload and being drawn into the autonomic storm

---

165 Caldwell P (2011) *Autism and Intensive Interaction*. Training film. London: Jessica Kingsley.
166 Moskowitz AK (2004) Scared stiff: Catatonia as an evolutionary-based fear response. *Psychological Review* **111** (4) 984–1002.

that triggers the delays in motor processing. In this sense one might say that the cessation of activity, be it physical or cognitive, could be a strategic response to fear, since the descriptions of sensations that accompany the autonomic storm are terrifying: one child says, 'it's like having my head in a car crusher'.

Chapter eight:
A behavioural
approach?

Containment or cause?

From the point of view of care and support, one of the problems we face is that the intensity of such storms tends to focus the attention of the non-spectrum world on containment rather than causes: what do I do now, rather than how can I organise the environment in such a way as to reduce or eliminate the triggers to such outbursts?

Broadly speaking there are two approaches. If we return to Pranve, at one stage in our interaction he is in the hall banging the door, which his father says he does when he is angry, and they try and stop him. I suggest that rather than doing this, they respond instead – and I bang my feet on the floor. Almost at once Pranve starts to smile and comes into the sitting room where we are. His father says, 'I see that we have been trying to control him and you are always there for him', neatly summarising the difference between a behavioural and a therapeutic approach. One is based on ideas of containment and direction, and the other on tuning in and communication: an outside-in versus inside-out approach.

The proponents of behavioural approaches strongly believe in and stoutly defend their position. In the Auton case (*Auton v British Columbia* [2004] 3 SCR 657), the lawyer Chris Hinkson is quoted as saying, 'The inability to communicate is one of the hallmarks of autism. These children, left untreated, will be doomed to a life of institutionalisation and looking inwardly only.'[167] In disagreeing with this statement one needs to

---

167 Dawson M (2004) *The Misbehaviour of Behaviourists: Ethical challenges to the behaviourists* [online]. Available at: http://researchautism.net/autism_research_journal_articles_publications_study.ikml?ra=1587 (accessed January 2014).

distinguish between, on the one hand, 'functional communication', which exchanges information and addresses needs, and on the other, 'emotional engagement'. Although some may never learn able to speak, if one uses body language to communicate, virtually everyone can engage in profound affective interaction and express joy in doing so. As stress peels away, some do start to use language. With three of the children I have worked with, the first thing they have said to their parents is, 'I love you'.

However, there is no doubt that under certain circumstances behavioural approaches can work – but there are alternatives that are more respectful towards the individual and recognise the difficulties that underlie their behaviours. So I want to start by comparing Intensive Interaction and ABA (applied behaviour analysis). Putting aside the physical punishments which featured in the original form of ABA but are discontinued now, ABA does use both sanctions and support to modify unwanted behaviours and encourage socially desirable ones.

Both ABA (and Positive Behaviour Reward) and the therapeutic approach known as Intensive Interaction (see Appendix 2) aim to address the difficulties that a child on the spectrum has in relating to people and the environment, although they come at it from completely different starting places. But for either to be effective, they have to begin by claiming the child's attention.

Basically, behavioural management seeks to reprogramme the brain, manipulating and 'improving' behaviour and raising intellectual capacity through targeted management, generally promoting acceptable ways of social interaction and cognitive advancement. Underpinning this approach is the idea of adapting the child to the environment (since this is what the child will encounter), rather than the environment to the child.

In ABA[168], if a behaviour is deemed to be undesirable, such as one that interferes with the child's ability to attend, behavioural management looks at the activities of the child in terms of its antecedents, behaviour and consequences (ABC) and stimulus-response reward. Or, to put it more simply, what the child is doing and why they are doing it. However, while the 'why' addresses environmental responses, it does not necessarily take on board the neurological distress that underpins the unwanted behaviour. Furthermore, as in the case of emotional overload, the actual behaviour may not manifest at the time of its triggering but is suppressed until later,

---

168 See http://www.users.qwest.net/~tbharris/aba_handbook.htm (accessed January 2014).

so that there is no temporal relationship between the antecedent and its 'unacceptable' outcome.

In respect of autism, the premise that underpins behavioural management is flawed, since its judgements and strategies are designed on the basis of the sensory experience of the non-spectrum view point, whereas negative behaviour in those with autism is virtually always the outcome of sensory distress, which it overlooks. And in society's anxiety to guide a child towards 'normality' there is the danger of treating them as an object rather than an individual who may be subject to extreme sensory distortions and sometimes severe pain.

Suppose our target behaviour for a particular child, Carly, is that she should learn to sit still, we need to ask ourselves why she's constantly on the move. Carly's answer[169] is, 'I can't sit still because my legs feel as though they are on fire and there are hundreds of ants crawling up my arms. If I do not bang my head, it feels as if my body is going to explode. It's just like shaking a can of coke. If I could stop it I would but it's not just like turning off a switch... I want something that will [put] out the fire.' We need to address Carly's sensory experience before trying to get her to conform to our expectations.

Or take a child who attacks her teacher, trying to rip off her T-shirt. She may well be protesting at the colour or pattern which sets of visual disturbances that are painful. Far from attempts to manipulate her behaviour, when the teacher understands the nature of scotopic sensitivity and wears plain quiet coloured clothes, the child's negative behaviour is not repeated.

Professor Porges says, 'when we watch a person's body language, we are reading their physiological state'[170]. Using a child's body language to establish emotional engagement is an attempt see how a child is 'talking to themselves', or, to be more precise, what is the exact physical feedback they are giving themselves. So if a child is flapping their hand, we might flap our hand, or make a non-verbal sound that reflects the rhythm of their movement. This treats their activity as a language, engages their attention and allows us to build up an empathetic conversation, drawing their attention from solitary self-stimulation to shared activity. They become interested in and begin to interact with what is going on around them. By communicating in a way that is easy for the brain to process,

---

169 See http://www.youtube.com/watch?v=vNZVV4Ciccg (accessed January 2014).
170 Porges S & Buczynski R (undated) *Polyvagal Theory: Why this changes everything* [online]. Mansfield, CT: National Institute for the Clinical Application of Behavioural Medicine. Available at: www.nicabm. com (accessed January 2014).

stress is reduced on the processing system, allowing the brain to function more effectively. Such an approach does not require a targeted agenda but uses the individual child and the difficulties they are experiencing as the starting point.

Whereas behavioural modification seeks to adapt the child to its environment, Intensive Interaction is part of the process of adapting the environment to the child's distorted sensory processing. ABA presents as being more interested in the techniques of its approach than in the individual difficulties a child may be experiencing. At its most extreme, a care worker expressed this by saying of a child who was having difficulties when being forced to have a shower, 'he has to get through the pain barrier'. In order to adopt this attitude we should have to ignore the spoken description of another child who says that for her, having a shower is 'like having red-hot needles fired at her head'. In which case, an acceptable alternative is a bath. (Nevertheless in some cases the negative physiological experience is the other way round, showers are acceptable but baths are not. It is a question of finding out what it is that is interpreted by the brain as painful, sometimes overwhelmingly so.) If one is going to draw a behavioural line in the sand it is critical that we choose those behaviours that are essential, such as those that relate to personal safety, rather than those that are merely 'desirable' from a non-spectrum perspective. We need to avoid raising the stress levels as far as possible.

Intensive Interaction is at its most effective when combined with attention to the sensory distortions underpinning autism. In particular, we have only to look back at Mike's experience of being trapped in the slow lane of his special school until he was found to be experiencing the visual processing distortions characteristic of Irlen syndrome – and his subsequent removal to a school especially catering for clever children – to realise that we cannot accurately set a base line for cognitive improvement until the sensory issues have been addressed (see p39). For example, no matter how many rewards I am offered or how many sanctions are applied, I cannot respond to your directives if I cannot distinguish the target from its background.

However, if we do treat the child as an object rather than subject, it may sometimes be possible to teach them a target behaviour without being concerned as to what the child is experiencing – but at the same time we risk raising their stress levels. For example, a programme on TV some years ago followed a child through a successful behavioural learning programme, but at the very end one of the child's parents is left wondering why he has taken to going into the garden to strip leaves (ie. he has developed a repetitive compulsive behaviour).

Carlo Schuengal and his colleagues[171] measured the sympathetic stress level in a comparison between interventions where a therapist teaching adaptive behaviours to stressful situations established a relationship with a child, as compared with one where there was no relationship component. Stress levels were found to be significantly higher where no relationship was established.

In a more extreme response to behavioural intervention, Donna Williams tells us that such strategies may feel like a senseless ritual of abuse, regardless of good intentions.

Like many therapies, ABA has moved outwards from its original regimented training formulation to a more flexible approach that focuses on social communication in a variety of settings, since, 'research has not supported the effectiveness of traditional ABA practices in teaching social communication and other critical, functional skills'[172].

But the basic choice is still between compliance and engagement – and with ABA the pay-off is conditional. It is not really interested in the psychological impact of the behavioural approach and whether achieving the target may have secondary effects. As Herb Lovett put it, the subliminal message becomes, 'I'll love you if you're good, therefore I will not love you if you are not good, therefore you are not worth loving for yourself'[173]. This is true both whether the response to unacceptable behaviour is to 'ignore it' or to 'punish' it, or to reward the 'good' behaviour.

How well ABA works is still a matter of debate. Attempts to review its efficacy tend towards vigorous support by its proponents but more ambiguous independent analysis. The authors of a 2011 review concluded that:

'… although ABA approaches were associated with … improvements in cognitive performance, language skills, and adaptive behaviour skills', they also say, 'the strength of evidence … is low, many children continue to display prominent areas of impairment … subgroups may account for a

---

171 Schuengel C, Oosterman M & Sterkenberg PS (2009) Children with disrupted attachment histories: interventions and psychophysiological indices of effects. *Child and Adolescent Psychiatry and Mental Health* **3** (26).

172 Prizant BM (2009) Straight talk about autism. *Autism Spectrum Quarterly* (spring 2009).

173 Lovett H (1985) *Cognitive Counselling and People with Special Needs*. Westport, CT: Prager.

majority of the change … there is little evidence of practical effectiveness or feasibility beyond research studies and the published studies used small samples, different treatment approaches and duration, and different outcome measurements.'[174]

Not all behavioural approaches are so determinedly detached from the impact their therapies have on stress levels. But it does seem that a child must be sufficiently cognitively advanced in order to be able to relate cause and effect in order to benefit. And they may be so entrenched in a behaviour that they need to be removed from the background that is promoting it.

If the efficacy of ABA and similar approaches are therefore open to question, can we say with more certainty that Intensive Interaction works? Melanie Nind[175] discusses the case study of Kris who was very withdrawn and whose autism was diagnosed at age four. As an adult, changes in his behaviour were evaluated over the period of a year, during which time he received regular interventions of Intensive Interaction. Eye contact improved, he positioned himself more closely to his teacher and more frequently turned towards her. These results are supported by a similar study undertaken by Dundee University's psychology department, who used frame-by-frame analyses of filmed interventions. They conclude that while the timeline may vary, Intensive Interaction (using body language to communicate) *always* resulted in an increase in eye contact, promoted the desire for close contact and increased social responsiveness[176].

Within the limits of a learning disability, if present, the child or adult may also demonstrate that they can generalise and copy hand movements. Sometimes they start to use words appropriately as the stress is reduced and demonstrate interest in their partner's behaviour. Particularly when used in combination with attention to reducing stress triggers, as in the combined approach 'PAVE' (promoting autism faVourable environments)[177] (see p52), interaction normally starts as soon as the child's brain is presented with signals it recognises as being part of its repertoire, very often within 10 minutes of commencing the intervention.

174 Warren Z, Veenstra-Vander Weele J, Stone W, Bruzek JL, Nahmias AS, Foss-Feig JH, Jerome RN, Krishnaswami S, Sathe NA, Glasser AM, Surawicz T & McPheeters ML (2011) Therapies for children with autism spectrum disorders. *Comparative Effectiveness Reviews, No. 26.* AHRQ Publication No. 11-EHC029-EF. Rockville, MD: Agency for Healthcare Research and Quality.
175 Nind M (1999) Intensive Interaction and autism: a useful approach? *British Journal of Special Education* **26** (2).
176 Zeedyk S, Caldwell P & Davies C (2009) How rapidly does Intensive Interaction promote social engagement for adults with profound learning disabilities? *European Journal of Special Needs Education* **24** 119–137.
177 Bradley E & Caldwell P (2013) Mental Health and Autism: Promoting Autism FaVourable Environments (PAVE). *Journal of Developmental Disabilities* **19** (1) 8–23.

In practice, parents who adopt Intensive Interaction as part of the way they communicate come back and say, 'we've got happy kids now'.

As a matter of practice and of respect, and also on philosophical grounds, I prefer to work alongside a child or adult rather than through imposition, using motivation rather than coercion. But given that sometimes a behavioural approach can help, a useful question to ask is what is the common factor between a behavioural and a therapeutic approach that makes for successful intervention? However, before addressing this question, I want to listen to Chris, who is telling me about what her autism has meant for her and how she experiences the reality that we share.

Chapter nine: Living on the borders

Quiet places

There are still barren places in Britain, borderlands with few inhabitants, where the sky belongs to red kites and the hillsides to stumbling streams. Up here one can wander along forest tracks and come out on the top of a dissected plateau where there is space: space not just in the sense of wide horizons, but also from social pressure, from expectations and the need to be acceptable, to conform and not to be afraid of betrayal by a sudden awkward movement, a jerking arm that knocks a cup over. Here there is nobody to reject one.

I share this love of wild spaces with Chris, who first came to see me in Yorkshire to talk about her sons who are on the autistic spectrum. Our conversation got round to the difficulties in her life until it became evident that, although she has never been diagnosed, she also sits squarely in the middle of the spectrum: like a number of people in her position, her chaotic but unrecognised sensory experiences have been compounded by distressing life events. She has very generously agreed to share some of this sensory turmoil with me, so now I am on my way to meet her and her family in the remote area where she has settled.

Chris is 47. She has four children, two older daughters who are grown up and live away and two sons aged 14 and 11, who live at home. Her life has been difficult. When she was little, she told her mother about what she experienced. The response she received was that she should not tell anyone else as they would think she was mad. So she grew up with the burden and fear of this belief: fear that has become inbuilt; it is part of her life and at times paralyses her ability to act and respond.

Chris remembers this fear, even in her cot. She would cry in the dark, but when someone opened the door and there was a burst of light, the contrast between light and dark confused her vision, her eyes could not accommodate so she could not see who was coming in and was even more afraid. Not perhaps such an unusual childhood experience of darkness at night time, but the problems with bright light have persisted: she still finds it painful to look into the light and transitions from light to dark and dark to light disorientate her and make her feel vertigo. She cannot look at the horizon for any length of time, even if there is no sun. One eye is different from the other; it has different colour tones. Eye contact is difficult. Nowadays her visual distortions would almost certainly be diagnosed as Scotopic Sensitivity or Irlen syndrome – not confined to people with autism but more prevalent in those on the spectrum.

Aged four, when she told her mother she was afraid, her mother (who in retrospect Chris now believes was also on the autistic spectrum) told her that her bedroom was haunted by the ghost of her grandfather. Chris says that from four or five she realised she felt 'different'. At nursery school she got into trouble for telling a small girl that she was an alien from space and making her cry. She did not mean to frighten her but, like the boy in *A Bridge of Voices*[178] who tells us that he feels like an alien from a different world, this was how she felt herself to be. She did not belong.

Her feelings of alienation made her stand out. She describes the bullying at school vividly, as 'playing with my vulnerabilities'. She would walk to the next bus stop along the route to avoid getting hit or spat at by the ringleader, who gathered there, waiting for the school bus with her 'in' group.

Chris has learned not to trust what her senses are telling her, the feelings of touch sensors being fired when she is not being touched – 'like water on my leg, like a cat's paws walking along my skin' (she walks her fingers along her leg, and is very specific; not the same as the shivery, 'goose walking over my grave'). She has hearing distortions, tinnitus and 'deep compression', combined with changes in tone. Her head feels tender, 'like there is mobile fluid under the skin which hurts to the touch'. She hits the top of her head.

---

178 Weeks L (undated) *A Bridge of Voices.* Documentary audiotape, BBC Radio 4. Produced by Tom Morton for Sandprint Programs.

In addition to problems with processing visual, tactile and auditory information, she also has vestibular problems – 'sometimes I don't know which way I am up. When I put my head at a certain angle I lose my physical sense of self.' This caused her problems when she went rock climbing and had to lean her head out backwards, losing all sense of bodily connection. And always there are feelings of being watched: feelings that intensify when she is on her own and has nothing to distract her. Perhaps it is still her mother's critical eye, but 'it always feels like someone is in the room', 'my body feels on standby all the time'.

Chris used to tap a lot and was always being told to stop, so she doesn't do it now, but 'it's hard not doing it'. (She still enjoys the sensory stimulation of running her fingers across the pile of a velvet cushion, which she does while we are talking.) And she used to steal her mother's cigarettes when she went out to the garden and left one still smouldering on the mantelpiece, having a few quick puffs. She smoked regularly from the age of 10, now smokes roll-ups heavily, needing an activity to focus on.

Apart from processing problems of sensory stimuli, Chris also talks about her relationship to her body, how she has 'out of body' experiences when she is looking down on herself, observing herself from above, and having no relationship with her body, 'my head and body seem to separate'. (A small boy on the spectrum describes this to his mother as, 'my head's running away, my head's running away'.)

And there is a loss of boundaries: 'I don't know which bits are me; who I am and who everyone else is, is not clear – the edges between us seem to soften, sometimes they include everyone else rather than just me, I can't be separate'. Or:

- 'I find myself being fragments of other people.'
- 'But sometimes my body is too tight.'
- 'I can't see all of myself at the same time. Until I look in the mirror, I have no idea what I look like, who I am.'

Because of the sensory distortions Chris experiences, she says that when faced with a situation her first question now is always, 'is this real or not real?' 'Bits of me seem to have to be on the backburner so I can function at all,' she says, 'When I have lost my boundaries, the first puff of a cigarette [a physical sensation] brings everything back.'

In addition to all this, there is 'emotional overload' (used in the sense which I understand that Donna uses it – a bodily flooding of sometimes disconnected feelings, pure sensation without a home, the word 'emotion' not connecting with affective warmth; an internal effect rather than cause). This does not seem to be related to anything and is rather a floating time-bomb, activating without warning. 'Sometimes you know what you want to do but just can't do it: I will want to read but just sit crying, the page is just a string of words.' Her ability to attend and put things together has gone.

Chris says she will go through the motions of an activity because it is what is expected of her, but later is flooded with feelings, sometimes crying without knowing why, which she describes as, 'an amplification of the emotion'. It is difficult to hold her overwhelming feelings in and she finds herself shaking with the effort. 'When this becomes extreme it's totally full on, you can't turn it off, you can be angry inside and it just bursts out.' (Like William's Anger Box. And, like William, when she describes this she presses her arms down towards her fingers, says it feels as though she is trying to get rid of it. We agree that in terms of body language it has the same urgency as Lady Macbeth's attempt to wipe the blood from her hands.)

Or emotions can be misdirected, pointing to the wrong source. With other people's feelings she is not good at reading their body language, 'sometimes reading more into them than is there and getting the wrong idea'.

Since school, Chris worked with old people in a nursing home at nights and then in a garden nursery – she liked working in the potting shed on her own. But it is not that she doesn't like people, she has good friends, a number of them on the autistic spectrum, 'since even if we are not the same, we understand each other'. And then she tells me that 'somewhere along the line' she learned that she had to take responsibility for herself, 'that feelings that I thought were from the outside world were actually my own feelings'. She had cognitive behavioural therapy, which she says reduced what had happened as a consequence of her sensory perceptions (misperceptions?) but could not remove the sensations themselves. But she was able to re-evaluate them. And an Indian guru helped her, giving her a strong new name since her old name represented all the struggles she had had, re-christening her into a new life. She uses it with friends and feels comfortable with it.

But fear and anger still stalk her life. In the struggle to be perceived as normal, she has problems going out, even shopping at the local Co-op, in case she does not walk straight down the aisle but, like Mike (see p39), she veers from side to side and people will notice she is 'odd'.

'I am so clumsy; my hand jerks and I spill a cup of tea. I knock and bash myself all the time, I'm covered with bruises and cuts.' I ask her if she self-harms and she answers with a touch of irony, 'I don't need to, it happens to me all the time without me trying'.

Chris is afraid of failure. 'I'm afraid that if things are not done in a certain way I will fail and then I shall stick out and not be normal and people will notice.' And then she says that 'you almost see yourself eroded and it's going to let you down so you don't do things'. And she is frightened of making commitments in case she can't fulfil them and lets people down.

Anger is also her companion. Sometimes it gets so bad that, in an effort to hold it in check, she has to say to her children, 'don't talk to me now', and they know it is better not to.

But when I look at how Chris and I use the word 'anger' I realise that it has different connotations. I am 'angry with', or 'angry about, or at' but for Chris, her anger does not always appear to have an immediate cause, but is endogenous, free floating, part of the fabric of her life. In spite of this, she tells me that although it does not immediately appear to be related to an event, she notices it does seem to surface when she is put in the position of having to attend to several things at once. For example, she cannot cook and talk at the same time. Multi-tasking is just too much of a processing demand.

Some writers distinguish between anger and rage. Sue Parker Hall[179] suggests that the latter is a deeply buried attempt to summon help by an infant who experiences terror and whose very survival feels under threat. She argues that its origins are in a pre-verbal, pre-cognitive, psychological defence mechanism, arising in earliest infancy in response to the trauma experienced when the infant's environment fails to meet their needs. Such rage is too deeply buried to be accessible to cognitive therapy, which relates to Chris's experience that while it enabled her to come to terms with the outcomes of her behaviour, it still left her with the raw affect.

In a meltdown or autonomic storm, adrenalin and cortisol, with all their affective effects, are on the rampage. At this stage, there is nothing that the

---

179 Parker Hall S (2009) *Anger, Rage and Relationship: An empathic approach to anger management*. Hove: Routledge.

sufferer can do to regulate their behaviour. And just as puberty affects boys particularly, the menopause with its hormonal surges has made this worse for Chris over the last two years.

Both small and big decisions can be paralysing for Chris in case she gets the answer wrong. The size of the decision makes no difference. She says it is 'like she gets separated from the answers, the questions are here but the answers are out there. There's a gap like it's a physical sensation.' This affects her family, for example, when her children ask her what they are going to do today – she sometimes cannot make a choice, so they stay at home doing nothing.

'You dread things that should be enjoyable', she says. But in spite of this she is sometimes able to make herself do something she knows will be hard, such as going to a party. While she does not take drugs herself, she says, 'it is easier if other people are spaced out because they become disinhibited and the barriers come down and they are easier to relate to. They don't mind if you're a bit weird, they just think you are high and accept your difference.'

I stayed the night with Chris and her family. The following day, five of her friends with autism came, bringing their lives with them, one after the other stories of adoption, rejection, desertion and sometimes anger interwoven with fear – fear of failure engendered by the pressure they experience from society to be seen to be 'normal'. All have gravitated independently to, and chosen to live in, this under-populated countryside in what, to an outsider, might be seen as an 'alternative life-style', tending to keep to themselves mainly because of the pressure they experience from the expectations of non-spectrum society.

'Social acceptability'

Talking to individuals in the process of writing this book has brought me into the company of many more articulate individuals on the Asperger's end of the spectrum than those who I normally meet. It has also made me very aware that the non-spectrum drive for achieving social acceptability (with its disregard for the sensory distortions and pain that people on the spectrum are having to cope with) is a double-edged sword. The pressure it places on people on the spectrum is compounding their autistic struggles to make sense of their environment. A National Autistic Society (NAS) paper on anxiety and Asperger's syndrome states that, 'People with Asperger's syndrome are particularly prone to anxiety disorder as a consequence of the social demands made upon them'[180]. It relates the onset of symptoms of catatonia, slowness affecting movement and speech and verbal responses, and difficulty in initiating or completing tasks, to mental illness. But Damian Milton, himself on the spectrum, sees his behavioural manifestations of freezing, excitement, agitation and an increase in repetitive behaviour as indicative of stress or excitement related to the social environment he finds himself in. He says, 'these descriptions are not indicative of mental illness but behavioural manifestations of my autistic disposition'.

Damian continues:

'another interpretation of the onset of such behaviour could be the resultant stress of being an autistic person in contemporary society, being hopelessly misunderstood by the psychiatric 'gaze'. The two-pronged attack of the medical model and (cognitive behavioural) psychological narrative has done great damage to autistic people and takes attention away from the social conditions that autistic people find themselves in – and the disadvantaged position such ways of thinking place autistic people in. The narrative of "behavioural management" also supports a damaging social ideology regarding disability.'[181]

The balance between society's urgent demand for 'normality' and the sensory pressures of autism is extremely delicate. We are in the position where any behaviour that deviates from the norm is seen as unacceptable and must be 'corrected'.

How does this social pressure translate in simple terms in the life of an 'autistic family'?

In their forceful paper entitled *The Normalisation Agenda and the Psycho-Emotional Disablement of Autistic People*[182], Milton and Lyte challenge the legacy of Lovaas and recent attempts to modify the techniques he recommended. 'By offering educational interventions as being capable of producing 'normal' functioning,' they argue, 'Lovaas was seriously underestimating the biological conditions that influence the expression of autistic behaviour patterns and the difficulties that autistic people with normal

---

180 NAS (2011) *Mental Health and Asperger Syndrome* [online]. London: National Autistic Society. Available at: www.autism.org.uk/working-with/health/mental-health-and-asperger-syndrome.aspx (accessed January 2014).
181 Milton D (2012) The normalisation agenda and the psycho-emotional disablement of autistic people. *Autonomy, the Critical Journal of Interdisciplinary Autism Studies* 1 (1).
182 *Ibid.*

IQ measures and educational placements can have with their impairments and with the social expectations and structures imposed upon them.'[183]
Lyte describes how, 'he [Milton] had to survive in a culture he simply could not make sense of ... and his unrealised intellectual and creative potential were causing him indescribable misery'. 'I became a frightened, passive prisoner in a world I was alienated from by their violent attempts to avoid seeing who I really was and what I may contribute to humankind.' He continues, 'I can confirm that a great part of my life has had to be concerned, at incalculable personal cost, with the literally vital need to reclaim my disempowered self'.

As they grow up, Wendy Lawson talks about, 'the lack of opportunities that autistic people have in society, coupled with the social stigma of being seen as having a pathologically deviant cognition is added to further by the trauma of passing as normal'[184].

However, change is tentatively in the air. A German international software firm, SAP, is actively recruiting people on the spectrum with IT skills to give it an advantage over its competitors, since those with autism are much faster than neurotypicals at spotting flaws in software and programmes. Research has shown that their memory and attention to detail definitely give them the edge over their non-spectrum colleagues. Offices are being adapted, there is little sound and low level of lighting and neurotypical colleagues are taught to respect difficulties that people with autism might have doing such things as shaking hands.

SAP intends to employ 650 people with ASD by 2020. Nor is it the only global business firm that is recognising the particular skill set of some people on the spectrum, signalling, according to a *New Scientist* article, a shift in society's perception of the condition[185].

However, autism manifests at all levels of cognitive development, and as the same *New Scientist* article points out, 'not all people on the spectrum would find such jobs suitable. It does, however, signal a greater acceptance of autism in society'. Talent and skill recognition are a beginning. Particularly, the tone of the article is one of respect.

---

183 Sainsbury C (2000) *Martian in the Playground: Understanding the schoolchild with Aspergers syndrome*. Bristol: Lucky Duck.

184 Lawson W (2008) *Concepts of Normality: The autistic and typical spectrum*. London: Jessica Kingsley.

185 Hodson H (2013) Neurotypicals need not apply: have autism, will travel. *New Scientist* **1 June**.

For families of less able children, facing the autistic imponderables does arouse in them an atavistic concern that they may not be able to cope in the world in which they are growing up. And for those who are at the least able end of the spectrum, they are right to be worried, since we are still a long way off meeting their support needs, both in the physical and, perhaps even more so, in the psychological sense. When will they speak? What can I do if my child has a meltdown in the shops? What will people think? How will my child manage if they are rejected by society? Who will look after them? For these parents, the idea that somehow autism can be 'fixed' is more than just attractive but uttered out of desperation.

In some ways, however, provision for the less able is not quite so challenging as for those on the Asperger's end of the spectrum, since it is they who are most able who are going to come into contact and be aware of misunderstanding with society in general, a society who, ignorant of the way the autistic brain is processing information, may interpret responses as rude or threatening. For example, while at school, Rubin continually asked the same question because he was not getting an answer that exactly matched the question he asked (and was told he was being cheeky). But Temple Grandin says she repeatedly asked, 'the street lights are coming on aren't they?' in order to get the same answer over and over again. And Naoki Higashida[186] says he hears an answer but does not remember it. Given the struggle for coherence, three perfectly logical but different reasons for repetition (accuracy, predictability and short-term memory loss) converge towards what is seen by the non-spectrum world as a 'compulsive behaviour' and marks out the perpetrator as somehow 'different'.

Coming back to Chris and her friends, living on the edge, on the borderlands of society in both the physical and the psychological sense, is protective, a place where it is relatively possible to maintain identity without pressure to conform. In this context we talk about hippies and whether at least some are 'autistic refugees' from society. I asked them how they had met, and they said they had recognised each other, even across the street, it was just easy to say 'hello' because you knew at once that here was someone who would not judge you.

Next, they asked me why I had come, was it because they were 'interesting'? I had to think: well, no and yes, was my response – no in the academic sense that I was not wishing to inspect them through a microscope, but yes

186 Higashida N (2013) *The Reason I Jump: The inner voice of a thirteen-year-old-boy with autism*. London: Sceptre.

– when I had met Chris she had been open about her sensory difficulties. Since it is important that non-spectrum and spectrum people understand each other, I had asked if we might talk. We have to take every opportunity to learn from each other.

Before I left, Chris said our meeting had made a difference to them. She explained that it had given them a language they could use to talk to each other about their sensory and psychological experiences. Whereas before they had tried to share their distress, now they had words that could act as a framework to convey and share meaning more effectively, an anchor for the empathy they have for each other. And they do mean empathy. When there is no fear of rejection Chris is deeply aware of and can tune in to the feelings of others, even if she is sometimes over-affected by them.

What I have learned from this articulate group of people is respect, or rather looking at respect for difference in an alternative way. To illustrate this I am going to have to leave Chris and her friends and turn to a young man whose autism is compounded by very severe learning disabilities. He has no speech and makes no contact with his surroundings, wandering around twiddling his hands and feeling his belt. Classically, his expression would be described as 'living in a world of his own'. When I use his breathing rhythm to make contact with him, he comes and stands very close, touching my face with his hands, running his fingers over my cheeks and forehead and feeling my lips and teeth, much as a blind person might explore the features of one who is engaging their attention. (For there is a sense in which he does not see me, that is, he is not making connection with what he sees, his visual experience has no meaning for him.) When he has felt my face, he feels his own. He becomes 'switched on', radiant, and keeps coming back to me. His teacher remarks that she had never seen him 'want to be with people' before.

Now that he has left school I learned recently that in his current service the policy is for staff in the community home where he lives to interpose themselves between him and visitors to the house, holding their hand flat between his body and the visitors, telling him to 'Stand back': all in the name of socially acceptable behaviour.

It is true that when I first saw him in school, it felt momentarily as though he was coming uncomfortably close. But putting aside my feeling that he was invading my personal space gave him the opportunity to make contact with another human being. From the joy his body language expressed,

I suspect that, as he felt my cheeks and then his own, this was a rare occasion when in the middle of sensory chaos he was able to differentiate his feeling of 'self' from 'other than self' and embody that affect. Feeling my flesh and recognising it in his own, he knew himself as a separate person but also part of a commonality.

It is difficult for us, whose lives are defined by our boundaries, to understand how powerful such recognition is, since we cannot relate to others until we know who we are ourselves. Like the look-out on Columbus's starving ship shouting from the yard-arm, 'Land ho!', such urgency to relate is fundamental to the human condition, a survival imperative. We need each other. Those of us who fail to acknowledge such a need are psychologically living on a flat-earth[187].

So what do we mean by respect? I have deliberately left this young man unidentified, since I am not aiming my question at the individual support staff who work with him but rather at a mistaken service policy, which while it talks about respect, does not recognise the sensory turmoil that has led him into total withdrawal from a world where his efforts to make contact are rejected, placing its needs over and above his. It is after all his space, his home, and yet we still put our personal comfort above his need for embodiment, to know who he is. So he is alone. Each time we do this, we drive him further back into the experience of isolation. It is not too strong to say that in confusing 'respect' with 'respectability' we are damaging people who are defenceless.

As a society, we are only just beginning to look at the talents of the more able people on the spectrum, but we are also insensitive to the psychological needs and distress of some of those we support whose needs are greatest, unaware how our ignorance exacerbates the turmoil in which they live.

---

187 In sailing eastwards from Portugal towards what he thought was the East Indies, Columbus set out to prove that the earth was round. Although he was wrong in assuming the land he had discovered in 1492 was the East Indies, his voyages opened up Europe to the New World.

Chapter ten: One thing at a time

Monotropism and attention

Returning to the question posed at the end of Chapter 8, at the heart of both behavioural approaches and Intensive Interaction is a desire to claim attention so as to move from isolation to engagement: this is in the belief that the ability to relate and to enjoy relationship is a fundamental part of what it is to be human. At the same time we have to recognise that not only do almost all people on the spectrum have problems processing speech but they may also be limited in the quantity of incoming stimuli that the brain can deal with. In this case they may only be able to deal with information supplied by one sense or one input at a time. For example, they may hear but not see, or see but not feel. Or, like Chris, they may be able only to cook or talk, but not both at once.

The term 'monotropism' highlights this difference between those on the autistic spectrum and non-spectrum people. 'At any one time, the [total] amount of attention available to a conscious individual is limited.'[188]
It suggests that autistic people show 'attention tunnels' with a deep interest in a narrow range of activities, as opposed to the experience of non-spectrum people, who show many interests in a less highly aroused form. This means that while autistic people may find it difficult to multitask, they may be very good at work that requires concentrated attention to detail.

While monotropism is advanced as a cognitive consequence of autism, rather than a cause, it needs be seen as an outcome of the brain's restricted ability to process the multitude of stimuli by which we are all bombarded. In addition to the goods yard rail analogy used earlier, I find it helpful to think of it as a metaphorical bottleneck caused by road works, where the stop/go

---

188 Murray D, Lesser M & Lawson W (2005) Attention, monotropism and the diagnostic criteria for autism. *Autism* **9** (2).

man has decided to ease congestion by letting through only red cars. Or blue ones. One sense at a time. Frustrated in my grey car, I shall reflect that the first cause of this hold-up in flow lies not so much in the controller's bizarre reasoning but in the constriction caused by lane closure – as was suggested in Chapter 3 in a discussion on competition between climbing fibres bearing mixed incoming stimuli to a reduced number of Purkinje cells.

Moving on

Having listened to Chris, I want to ask now how it is that some people on the autistic spectrum do themselves appear to manage to learn to co-exist with their autism in what presents to them as a threatening environment? What strategies do they employ? Not that the autistic distortions have disappeared (as Chris has told us, her body is on standby all the time) but attention seems, at least at times, to have shifted away from the ensuing turmoil, so that in varying degrees people have come to terms with their sensory distortions.

First, we have to remember that autism affects people of all levels of cognitive ability and that there is neither one problem nor one solution. It depends exactly how differently the brain is wired and where these neurological differences and distortions have taken root. For example, even though the organs of sight and sound may be intact and functional, a person who is at the severe end of the spectrum may at times be unable to process their visual or auditory intake at all – and therefore not even see or hear the individual who is trying to intervene in their lives.

Second, these sensory distortions will manifest differently in each individual – each has their own sensory profile, which needs to be addressed before trying to decide where their cognitive baseline lies.

Third, due to the degree of social acceptance, or rather lack thereof, and the consequent pressure to conform, there may be a whole number of psychological problems and traumas overlying the autism which are being missed or dismissed as features of autism. It is critical that we listen to and pay attention to the person's psychological state (as manifested either verbally or through their body language) as well as their physiological difficulties.

And quite often it is not just the person who is involved, but 'this-individual-in-relation-to-this-particular-environment' that underpins behaviour affecting those with whom they live. For example, a child may be unable to cope with the sensory demands of a sibling who they perceive as 'winding them up' by the particular sounds they make. These may not just be irritating but, in the case of autism, actually painful. Alternatively, the sensory overload that accompanies school with its bells and multitude of people moving and speaking and the pictures on the walls, the general hustle and bustle, may be more than the individual can handle. There are times when it is necessary to remove a person from such a situation. (Particularly difficult to process are the brightly coloured wallboards with wavy edges covered with work and pictures. These are currently to be found in almost every school in the country. Attractive to the non-spectrum viewer, they add to sensory overload of the autistic child.)

What they need most of all is a sensory environment that is predictable so they are not overwhelmed by 'nonsensical' stimuli.

Shifting the balance

Is there anything that we in the non-spectrum world can do to help shift the balance in favour of a meaningful connection with the outside world, to make it more user-friendly? Especially for those who are struggling both with intellectual disability as well as autism?

If we try and reduce self-stimulation and its consequent inward focus, we are removing the protective shield they have developed against sensory distortion, making it more difficult for them to relate to the world outside and exposing them to the danger of the autonomic storming of which they are so afraid. However, there are more subtle ways of establishing a bridge by using their self-stimuli (the way they are talking to themselves), or if they are more able, to access their cognitive capacities, themes and interests, to make contact with them. We do this by placing ourselves alongside their interests and without increasing their processing difficulties, inserting a focal point sufficiently familiar and compelling as to redirect attention from the inner lockdown to a source of 'their personal vocabulary' that is coming from outside themselves.

But before embarking on this approach and in view of observations by some people with autism, we need to ask ourselves whether the whole idea of redirecting attention to the world outside is helpful and not patronising. Are there indications that they may want to sit life out where they are? Not surprisingly given the range of the spectrum, attitudes to the desirability of their relationship with their inner world are not uniform, varying from O'Neill's suggestion[189] that this is a calm state and they should be left to enjoy it, to William's more ambiguous view expressed when she discusses her poem *Nobody Nowhere*[190]:

'The room is the mind, it has no windows and you don't see out any more.'

Here, she says, 'you have all the relationships in there that you should have outside, you live in fear. You can visit in freedom but you live in it in fear'. On the other hand, Carly is very emphatic about people allowing her to continue her repetitive rituals, Milton describes his son as having a dynamic connection to the sensory world, but he continues that sometimes the sensory experience they live in is so chaotic that they seek out structure and routine to impose upon it, either derived internally or from outsiders.

Nevertheless, I would suggest that those people with autism who find the whole idea of intervention involving their stimming repugnant have as children only encountered negative interference, when well-intentioned support systems have tried to stop them pursuing repetitive behaviour (which is sometimes mistakenly believed to be obsessional compulsive disorder) and not to use them as a ladder to climb into a world where communication can be desirable.

In practice, when we do use a child or adult's individual repetitive behaviours or themes as elements of a language, tuning in to how a person feels, they are a passport to empathy and as such immediately attract positive responses of eye contact, smiling and interest. Described in an email by Josh as 'having a delicious conversation when his brain was becoming confused,'[191] when one embarks on such an intervention it immediately becomes clear that not only is it not seen as intrusive, but on the contrary it is virtually always welcomed. Suddenly there is a source out in the world beyond the turmoil, one that is easily recognised. Attention is engaged.

Being with

How do we start? Personally I will be bearing two principles in mind: first, the individual concerned, and second, the individual as part of their environment, including their reactions to supporters and supporters'

---

189 O'Neill JL (1999) *Through the Eyes of Aliens*. London: Jessica Kingsley.
190 Everson S (1995) *Jam-Jar*. UK: Fresh Film. (Film)
191 Caldwell P (2012) *Delicious Conversations*. Hove: Pavilion Publishing.

reactions to them. Normally asked to work with people or services who are in crisis, I want to see them in their normal environment. To begin with I usually talk to staff for a short while, enquiring where they feel the difficulties in care lie and if there is anything particular that is likely to upset them. I then move on to see the individual concerned. Contrary to established practice, I do not spend much time in observation but rather move in gradually, distancing my moves by the reactions I obtain, while observing the rule of thumb that I need to try and engage with them before moving in to their personal space. As if I were going to have a conversation with a friend, I do not stand around looking at them for some time first, since this can be interpreted as threatening – but I take our interaction as it comes. The reason for this is that in order to flow like a dialogue, my responses have to be contingent, answers to what is happening now rather than based on a pre-observed agenda.

Nevertheless, we need to start with ourselves and our own attitude. I cannot really express this better than by quoting an excerpt from *The Little Book of Behaviour* sent to me recently by James Clark and reproduced in full with his permission[192]. While I cannot agree with all his strategies, his account of how he learned to be with someone and share their space rather than trying to impose his own agenda is both tender, moving and enlightening:

'When I first started working with other people I was fortunate enough to work with an individual who taught me a rather wonderful lesson. The challenging behaviour that he exhibited was not of anger or aggression but of a perceived lack of interest, a want to do very little or so it seemed. On more than a few occasions members of staff would roll their eyes when they were informed they would be working with this young chap, and I freely admit I was one of them. You see, sitting in a room with nothing happening and no one talking, for up to and sometimes over an hour, can be quite a challenge. It was on one such shift I thought I would try to see what he found so interesting, try to follow his gaze and puzzle out what kept him in one place for so long. The more I looked the more I saw, stands to reason really! We could be sat outside and I found myself staring at leaves, wondering how the physics of the situation was taking effect, or just in the artistry of the movement. The more I appreciated the time I spent with him, the more I appreciated him as an individual (something I mistakenly thought I already did). This did not happen overnight, a wave of peace and calm did not wash over me and take me off to a magical place

---

192 Clark J (2012) *The Little Book of Behaviour.* Peterborough: Upfront Publishing.

where everyone's hats are made of chocolate! It took time, and anyone who knows me knows that simply sitting still is an act of will, which made this all the more challenging. You see when you spend time with someone and your mind is elsewhere then you're not really with them, in fact you're only occupying the same space. So it is not enough to just give time, after all what is time without meaning? Learn to enjoy what you're doing and thereby demonstrate to the other person that they are cared for because they can see it reflected in you. There is beauty in almost everything, we just have to look. I realised this as after a shift I found myself doing some washing, watching the various items vying for a position at the window, I must have stared at it for ages just enjoying the sound and the images made up of bubbles, water and cloth. As I gained more experience I began to understand that I found being in such a quiet situation challenging because I was faced with myself, no conversation, music or television for distraction. Confronting this helped build confidence and helped me understand that you don't have to fill the room, there is nothing wrong with silence. This can be so important when working with an individual who is easily overwhelmed, so many times I have seen well-meaning individuals use too much speech, too much movement and body language, just wait and relax. Start to build trust through understanding. You can't force the snow from the sky, but you can be patient.'

James learned from the resident he was supporting. He laid aside his own discomfort at not 'doing' something with him in favour of 'being with' him. Most people do find this difficult since we are programmed towards 'busyness'. The whole point of services is to fill the days of individuals with activity, regardless of what it is that they experience as meaningful, or in some cases threatening.

I am not suggesting that we sit around in idleness. 'Being with' is an active process that demands our full attention. I clearly recall the moment of switching my attention from 'boredom', or perhaps 'suspended focus', to full-on attention to what my partner found so fascinating about a bead slung on a string and discovering a whole new world of sensory impressions that had hitherto passed me by[193]. We have to be totally present to our partner's presence, working in the here and now. But once we are tuned in, we can carry the consequent sense of reciprocal relationship into all that we do with them. It will change both our lives.

---

193 Caldwell P (2006) *Finding You Finding Me*. London: Jessica Kingsley (p146).

Chapter eleven:
Listening in

Subjectivity

When I first started working with people on the spectrum, I was told by one hospital psychologist that it was a waste of time trying to find out about their autism by talking to them because their brains did not work properly, so what they had to say would be distorted and unscientific. Forty-five years on this blinkered view has changed. In her new book, Temple Grandin[194] takes us on a slice-by-slice tour of her formidable intelligence and tells us that if we want to understand people with autism, we should ask them. Laying aside the idea that such accounts are subjective and therefore unreliable, she emphasises that subjectivity is the whole point, we need to learn from what it is people with autism are experiencing. But, given that it is a spectrum as wide as that exhibited by the rest of us, it's not surprising that when we pursue this line, what we learn is of diversity and a graded response to internal emotional hypersensitivity stretching from the armour-plated to the totally exposed.

Nowadays, more and more people are beginning to talk about their autism and how they feel. The two great pioneers of self-advocacy, Temple and Donna Williams (who says non-spectrum people should stick our own reality in our back pockets and become anthropologists)[195], are both highly articulate but their brains' responses to affective overload leads them to adopt completely opposite strategies. Temple is an engineer, who quite literally builds walls to guide potentially frightened cattle to the slaughter-house in such way that they are unafraid. 'Feeling safe' is built into her designs. Donna's response is that of an artist and poet who, without regard to self-protection, transforms her personal landscape into creative insight, as reflected through her poems, books and paintings.

194 Grandin T & Panek R (2013) *The Autistic Brain*. Boston, MA: Houghton, Mifflin and Harcourt.
195 Everson S (1995) *Jam-Jar*. UK: Fresh Film. (Film)

Listening

Earlier I mentioned Porges, who is telling us that, 'when we listen to a voice we are listening to a person's physiological state'[196], but I should want to amend this to, 'we are listening to both their physiological and psychological state', although perhaps some might argue that this is an oversimplification and the two are deeply entwined, one reflecting the other. Our histories and responses are written not only into what we say but how we say it.

People like Chris can tell us about their lives but there are many others, less articulate, whose stories are written only in the way they make their sounds or the phrases they repeat. Some are exceptional mimics, not in the sense of deliberately using intonations and phrases as mockery, but when placed in situations that they find stressful, producing with extraordinary accuracy the verbal assaults they have endured previously in similar instances. Through them we hear the voices of those in whose care they have been placed – one cannot say by whom they were supported since these vocal vignettes are almost always negative, critical or repressive, with no understanding of what has led up to a particular behaviour. If we listen, we will hear the history of verbal misunderstanding and abuse to which some have been subjected: accurate echoes of the voices from their past.

Voices from elsewhere

Mario now lives in a very caring service where carers and those they support live together, sharing their lives in every sense. With infinite patience and recognition of his sensory problems, his life is gradually being transformed from one of desolation to acceptance. This is not an easy task since his early experience is deeply embedded: his negative responses still surface whenever he loses track of what is happening. It is not just the tone of his voice but the actual words he uses that convey to us so clearly the totally negative exasperation of previous carers.

When I first see him, Mario is 44. He has severe autism and lives in a house with two other residents and three live-in assistants, each of whom have been with him over at least a year.

Mario has not had a happy background and this can make him difficult to live with. Although his behaviour has shown improvement, he still gets

---

196 For more information, see www.youtube.com/watch?v=8RKC3Ga6shs (accessed January 2014).

acutely distressed, becoming aggressive towards others and to himself. When he is upset, he hits out, bites (himself or others), scratches, pinches, breaks glasses, bangs his head or thumps his fist. He puts his fingers in his ears when there are too many people around and especially if they are talking over him. He is acutely anxious and dependent on routine. He likes tea and wants it frequently.

While he can look after himself, give himself a bath and, given time, carry out the domestic routines of cleaning his room, laying and clearing the table and making tea, it is clear that Mario is experiencing acute sensory distress. He is sensitive to light, screws up his eyes at times and chooses the colour brown for preference. He needs physical pressure: at meals, he pulls his chair until he is squeezed tightly between it and the table. On occasion he will ask for a hug but his can be too strong and become painful. He is sensitive to smell, will smell people's shoes, even rub his fingers on them and smell them.

Mario has many mannerisms. He rocks and gets stuck rigidly in positions, looking at his extended hands and backwards and forwards from his hand to the cup which he carries much of the time. While he is in this semi-catatonic state, his brain is unable to issue the motor instructions to move on.

Mario hums and makes sounds and seems to live in the past, saying such things as, 'the cupboard fell on my head' or 'someone pushed me into the water'. His memories seem to float in and out of the present. He is confused between what is happening now and what has happened some time ago, leading him to say that one of the people he lives with at present did such and such a thing[197], when the incident actually happened in the distant past. On the whole he does know about sequence but is acutely anxious about intervals and when events are going to happen, particularly when people are coming or going.

Much of Mario's verbal communication is dominated by whether or not he is being 'good' or 'bad', and in the past he has learned to try and manipulate situations by echoing behavioural strategies that have been applied to his conduct: 'if I am good I will get a cup of tea'. He is very sensitive to emotional atmosphere and will lash out if there is an unhappy feeling around or he feels someone is afraid or not well.

---

197 Williams D (1992) *Nobody Nowhere: The remarkable autobiography of an autistic girl*. London: Jessica Kinglsey.

An aspect of autism that complicates our understanding is that it is easy for a person to adopt learned phrases and language. We are so anxious for them to speak that we often fail to grasp that there may be discrepancies between what they say and the meaning that this has for them or, as with Mario, its temporal relevance. We can also mistake what they say for their own thoughts or messages, when actually they were reprimands made by other people (often in traumatic circumstances) carrying the negative emotional charge of a situation. For example, if one joins in with Mario's hums or sounds, he will say, 'don't sing' or 'don't hum'. This may be that he wishes one to stop, but the voice he uses sounds more like someone else's, as if it is an echo of the past: when he hears humming and singing from someone else, he recognises it in the world outside his inner world and repeats what was said to him. Alternatively, if staff join in his rocking, he will take note and then start rock more furiously. It is as if he is desperately resisting being drawn out of his inner world to the world outside him, it is just too threatening as he perceives it.

Another related feature of people with autism's behaviour is that under external pressure they themselves can develop split persona which are noticeable as quite different voices, in particular a 'good, socially acceptable voice' and a 'bad negative voice' that expresses how they 'feel'. These voices have quite a different tone. Feeling themselves to be bad, sometimes the 'bad voice' comes over in expressions and content that have been shouted at them. In Mario's case one can hear quite clearly, a good 'meek' voice, which is how he has been taught to engage with the world, and a violent voice that shouts at himself, for example when he is asked to help clean his room – 'dirty stuff all over the carpet', reflecting earlier incontinence. At this point he is very distressed.

Donna Williams describes the three personalities she adopted with three different voices to cope with different situations. In projecting herself into these personalities, she explains that she lost all sense of her self, to the extent that she was convinced that her image in the mirror was her real self, even trying to walk through the mirror to reach her self. In practice, many people with this multiple voice condition have an undue relationship with their reflection, either seeing their image as their 'good self' – and wanting to be close to it – or as their 'bad self', in which case they will abuse it or dislike it, as in Mario's case. He also dislikes seeing his image as a reflection in the window and it may also account for the fact that when he is upset he will break people's glasses (in which he sees his reflected image).

The question we need to ask is how we can best re-centre Mario's sense of his real self, neither of which show up in his defensive voices.

The problem lies with us in our non-spectrum reaction, in that we discourage the 'bad voice' with its socially unacceptable 'rude' language – and in so rejecting what they say, we tell the person that how they feel does not matter – and by implication, they themselves have no value. So, when he is shouting at himself as he cleans his carpet, I ask his co-worker Pat, to align herself with how Mario is feeling by saying to him, 'it must feel really dirty'. Immediately he straightens up, clearly surprised and looks her full in the face. He says, 'What?' His body language totally changes, his attention is fully engaged and at that instant both Pat and I feel we meet the real Mario and not one of his projected personalities. After a few seconds he retreats again into his adopted 'bad' (as he sees it) personality.

The approach being used here is to tune in to how a person feels – but in order to do so it is essential to use the actual words or phrases involved. Mere sympathy is not enough. In order to refocus his attention away from his distress and onto the world outside himself, he has to hear exactly what is on his mind coming from elsewhere. It is the jolt of surprise that redirects his interest.

It may not always work – it did not seem to be effective when he was complaining he felt cold and wanted a bath. Although thinking about this, the difference was that, at that time he was using his 'meek' voice and since his autonomic system appears to be all over the place, it is quite possibly his thermoregulation is playing tricks on him and he really does feel cold in spite of the room temperature being perceived as warm by us.

If we go along with and join in his muttered loop of phrases about whether he is good or bad, we simply reinforce the wedge that drives the split between good and bad personalities and hence his projection and introjection, since neither are the real Mario. As described above, it is more effective to align oneself with how he feels when he is using his 'bad' voice. Even if this only works occasionally, each time it does it will bring him into our world in a user-friendly way.

Some people who have a poor sense of their physical bodies have quite literally rooted it in a particular part of themselves (the place where they are scratching themselves for example), or in some other object.

Whereas Mario's voice betrays the voices of his unhappy past, Nicole (see p23 and p73), has projected her sense of self into her doll. In spite of loving care from her family, she finds engagement so difficult that she has retreated into the safety of connection through an intermediary. 'Zac' acts as an emotional shield, psychologically becoming Nicole's mouthpiece. Being a talking doll, she uses it to speak for her. However, she does use him to communicate 'affectively', even offering him to those people she likes.

I suggest that instead of talking to her directly, her family accept that this is where she feels herself to be and adopt the strategy of communicating with her through Zac. Although one might consider this a backward step, it has reduced Nicole's stress levels. For example, she was not eating well and losing weight. When her mother put her meal on the table, Nicole held Zac's arm out towards the plate. Her mother said, 'No Zac, you know you can't eat Nicole's meal'. Nicole's response was to laugh and tuck in to her food. And since the introduction of talking to Nicole through Zac, she now shows her affection directly by throwing her arms round people. She has started to say, 'I love you' to her grandfather.

It is clear that her biggest worry was having to go to school, which for her was extremely stressful to the point where most of her time was spent curled up in a chair asleep. Since her mother withdrew her, Nicole has become much more responsive. Before, she was difficult to get her out of bed. Now that she is not so worried she gets herself up, dresses and comes downstairs. It is now possible to cut her finger and toenails in an hour whereas before each foot had to be done on a different day. She goes to the toilet when asked and recently helped her mother bake a cake, an activity that would previously have been hopeless as she would spill the ingredients into everything.

Even if a person does not use speech in any way, listening to the feedback they are giving themselves (tapping into their conversation between the brain and body) gives us a clue as to where their attention is centred.

While Nicole had relocated her feeling of her self into her doll, Jenny's sense of self appears to be completely lost. She spends her time at the day centre peering out of the door or, if outside, through the fence. She does not appear to understand when told it is dinnertime, even when shown her meal on a plate. When I look at her, she is scratching her thumb with her forefinger. It seems to me that she is giving herself sensation at this point and this may be where she quite literally feels herself to be. Instead of asking her if she would like to have her dinner I say, 'would your thumbs like some dinner?' Without hesitation, Jenny turns round and goes to the dining area where she sits down and eats her meal.

To address Nicole other than through Zac, or Jenny other than through her thumbs, is to miss the target. The message simply does not get through, at least not sufficiently to trigger a response. Or maybe it is received but cannot link up with the motor system, so that the person knows that some action is required but cannot respond, which can be very stressful. At least Zac is able to go through the motions of speaking when Nicole wants to, even if the range of his mechanical phrases is limited and they are necessarily non-contingent.

Chapter twelve: Confirmation and sense of self

Loss of sense of self

This chapter looks in more detail at a difficulty described by a number of people with autism: the loss of their 'sense of self'. I want to explore quite what this means. Does it mean I would have no physical image of myself? Should I be aware of this absence, know that something is missing? And how can I relate to others if I do not know what I am, what my boundaries are?

These days a distinction is drawn between 'consciousness' and 'self-awareness', with consciousness defined as awareness of the body and its environment and self-awareness as a recognition of that consciousness. Or, as Ferris Jabr puts it[198], 'to be conscious is to think, to be self-aware is to realise that you are a thinking being and think about your thoughts'.

This simple Descartian definition (I think, therefore I am) leaves out the part played by the perception and registration in the brain of feeling and sensation. As a largely intuitive thinker (processor), I need to add, 'I feel sensations (stimuli that are perceived externally through my sense organs as well as the internal affective spin-offs these generate), and reflect on my feelings, turning inwards towards them, as in the practice of 'mindfulness'. But knowing that affective sensation can sometimes lead one astray, my brain then checks its intuitions against logical argument. As Donna Williams says, 'there are all different ways of thinking'[199].

---

198 Jabr F (2012) *Self-awareness with a simple brain* [online]. Scientific American Mind and Brain. Available at: http://www.scientificamerican.com/article.cfm?id=self-awareness-with-a-simple-brain (accessed January 2014).
199 Everson S (1995) *Jam-Jar*. UK: Fresh Film. (Film)

Jabr continues that neuroimaging studies suggest that, when we are thinking about our selves, recognising our image and reflecting on our thoughts and feelings – all forms of self-awareness – have traditionally been thought to involve the outer crinkly part of the brain, the cerebral cortex. But the idea that self-awareness requires an intact cerebrum has been thrown into doubt by studies of a man who lost a large part of this area. Although he can no longer form new memories, he does recognise his own image in the mirror, wiping a smudge off his nose (placed there previously without his knowledge) when he looks at himself in the mirror and wondering how it got there. So he not only recognises his physical image but reflects on its disturbed appearance.

But what people with autism seem to be talking about is very concrete – not recognising which bits of them make up their bodies. Or not feeling that the bits they see are joined up to them, make part of a whole.

To put it simply, autistic or not, in order to know who I am I not only need an image of myself but one which has well-defined boundaries. I lose this picture if I am not getting a correct image of myself due to low proprioceptive cues, or to poor processing of those that my brain does receive – for example, if my cerebellum is not functioning as well as it should. In Donna Williams's case, when sensorily overloaded her brain would shut down either seeing or feeling, to ease overload. She could then see *or* feel, but not both together, so she did not feel that the hand she saw was part of herself but rather a separate thing floating in front of her.

Some people on the spectrum may not have an integrated picture of themselves at all. For example, Tito[200], who has severe autism, says 'he sees himself in bits, a leg or an arm, and his spinning is to try and reassemble his parts as a whole'. He uses movement to get a sense of his self: he tells us that when he flaps his hands, 'I am calming myself. My senses are so disconnected, I lose my body. So I flap. If I don't do this I feel scattered and anxious ... I hardly realised I had a body. I needed constant movement, which made me get the feeling of my body'[201]. 'I try to move constantly,' he says, 'to be aware that I am alive and my name is Tito.'[202]

---

200 Mukhopadhyay TR (2008) *How Can I Talk if My Lips Don't Move?*. New York: Arcade Publishing.
201 Blakeslee S (2002) A boy, a mother and a rare map of autism's world. *New York Times* **19 November**. Available at: http://www.nytimes.com/2002/11/19/science/a-boy-a-mother-and-a-rare-map-of-autism-s-world.html?pagewanted=print&src=pm (accessed January 2014).
202 Mukhopadhyay T (2004) Geneva Centre for Autism International Symposium for Autism 2004, Toronto, Canada, November 10–12.

In the film *Autism and Intensive Interaction*, Oli, a schoolboy of 17, explores my face with his fingers and then touches his own. And then he laughs with pleasure. What he is doing is trying to relate what he sees outside himself (teeth, chin, cheeks, brow) to what he feels (his own teeth, chin, cheeks and brow), fleshing out his own image. Or to put it another way, he is recognising and embodying an external experience, putting together his visual and tactile senses, something we have learned to do on our mother's knee and subsequently do automatically – but for him, he needs this physical exploration. By exploring me he confirms his sense of self.

Lizzie screams violently every 40 seconds but calms when I respond empathetically to each utterance. After a while, she comes and sits opposite me, reaches across the table and describes an arc with her hands, as if she were drawing the shape of a rainbow. She then looks at me and carefully presses the shape she has created between us. Without touching her, I respond with my hands, pressing the imaginary semicircle she has drawn in the air, so that we establish where we are in relation to each other, sculpting the boundaries in space between us.

With both Oli and Lizzie, they and I are learning about ourselves in relation to an 'other than self', and if we find circumstances are favourable, it becomes possible to establish enough trust to move out of isolation. (When I am working with someone whose reputation is for aggression, developing this trust is as important to me as it is to them.)

Embodiment is crucial to knowing what we are. Damasio explains that the first message to my brain is about my surroundings and the second tells me about my body, that my eyes or ears etc. are receiving the message. It informs me about myself. But this is a murky area: if I have no idea what is physically myself, I am also not going to be able to make out my boundaries, where I stop and you begin. Not having a defined concept of 'out there' as distinct from 'in here' interferes with the possibility of relationship. My physical boundaries are more than just limits of myself, they mark the difference between me and not-me, so that without them I am not just unable to get a coherent picture of the world and of myself, but also of 'myself in relation to other'. I need boundaries in order to be able to reach across them.

One might ask if we need to know what we are and where we physically exist in order to know ourselves. After all, Donna says that when she loses her sense of self, she seeks her image in the mirror – as do a number of others – so there is an awareness of entity, even if it is only defined by its absence[203].

Boundaries and sense of self are set up not only by our physical awareness of our own bodies, but also, in a psychological sense, by how others respond or fail to respond to us. Turkle[204] describes going into a café where everyone else has their heads down, tucked into a smart phone or iPad as they sip their coffee. She says that although she does not know them, she actually feels their absence as tangible and as a matter of regret. On the relationship scale of on-line, default and delete, heads turned away signify active rejection: 'not only do I not want you, I prefer someone else'.

And in relating to each other, distance is important: people who do not know their boundaries make us feel uncomfortable. They come too close and we say they are invasive and flinch. They stand off or turn away and we say they are cold. We do not enjoy the company of people who seek over-proximity or, alternatively, do not trust us enough to come near. Our personal space is physically defined and we resent invasion and take lack of trust as a personal criticism.

If the shape of absence is defined by its boundaries (like fingertip exploration of a gingerbread cutter in the dark), high-tech communication is ring-fenced, attention is elsewhere, so there is no possibility of catching someone's eye or a chance smile. Aloneness is made patent. And in survival terms, to be alone is to have no back-up in situations of potential danger. Even hermits pack their laptops these days.

Back to the beginning

To begin with, getting born is about the most hazardous adventure we undertake. After our long sojourn in the womb and hazardous squeeze through the birth canal, we are delivered into paradox, the paradox of total dependence and simultaneous existential aloneness. Worse is to come: 'snip', and we are disconnected from our life support system.

You and me – and the rest of us – we've all done it. And no matter what our gender or the colour of our skin, most of us spend the rest of our lives trying to work out how we can best relate to each other in order to survive in what is essentially a hostile system. In spite of our longing for independence we

---

203 Caldwell P (2007) *From Isolation to Intimacy*. London: Jessica Kingsley.
204 Turkle S (2011) *Alone Together*. New York: Basic Books.

are also looking for reconnection and reconciliation to the safest system we will ever experience to confirm our own existence. We need each other.

Even when we think we like to be on our own, we are all of us dependent on a social system organised for our maintenance – the people who keep our sewage system clear, our roads mended, our water and electricity online and, unless we are totally self-sufficient (and not many are), supply us with food.

Those of us who are born with an intact capacity to relate are fortunate. In infancy we exercise this with increasing fluency on our mother's knee. All being well, we make sounds and movements and copy each other, luring each other on with smiles and evident pleasure. But there are some mothers who say that they knew there was something not quite right from birth, since their child was not interacting in the way they would expect – 'he would never look at me. Right from the start, I knew there was something wrong'.

More puzzling are those who meet all the normal developmental signposts but then suddenly nosedive back into autistic behaviour: progression goes into reverse, a failure in development that has been linked to the MMR vaccine. While this has been discredited, it is sometimes awkward trying to explain as coincidence the sudden regression that very occasionally follows immediately after the vaccination of a child who appears to be developing normally, especially where this shows up in siblings separated by time. In order to untangle this apparently different onset, I agree with Temple Grandin who suggests that when looking at the aetiology of autism, statistical analysis should be separating children who start off well and crash around the age of late two to three from those in whom it is evident from the earliest stages[205].

However arrived at, what seems to be common in autism is that we and our autistic children are failing to connect: either the dyadic skills have failed to develop, or the communication deficits surface at a later date (even if the pattern was set early on in foetal development). Ephraim[206], who introduced the idea of using body language to communicate in the 1980s, suggested it was a question of synchronicity; the baby was failing to develop the dyadic games with its mother and by the time it had matured sufficiently, the mother had tried, failed and given up.

---

205 Grandin T & Panek R (2013) *The Autistic Brain*. Boston, MA: Houghton, Mifflin and Harcourt
206 Ephraim GW (1990) *A Brief Introduction to Augmented Mothering*. Harperbury Hospital, Herts: Playtrac.

Now we have a baby who needs to relate but lacks the skills and a mother who has instinctively tried, found it doesn't work and stopped trying. So what is it that the dyadic relationship gives us? Why (and how) is it so vital?

Confirmation

Roughly speaking, the infant initiates a sound or action, the mother confirms this and the baby (eventually) moves on to try out an alternative. From our point of view, the critical part of this exchange is confirmation. Damasio[207] points out when we take in information it not only tells us about the object we perceive but also about the organ receiving it, that is, 'my eyes are seeing this object', 'my ears are hearing this sound'.

So perception of incoming stimuli not only tells us about the world outside but also gives us awareness of our own state. In practice, it confirms what we are doing, particularly so by setting off motor responses to the incoming stimuli, so that we 'feel' what we perceive. (Classically, if I see you yawn, my jaw will start to tickle and I shall probably end up yawning myself.) Even where these motor responses are suppressed, they do seem to register and help us to embody incoming signals so that the act of perception of the world outside simultaneously confirms our self-image.

However, one hypothesis is that the mirror neuron system is not working effectively in people on the autistic spectrum, so they do not recognise and receive the physical embodiment and therefore cannot respond[208].

This has to be qualified by the observation of practice, that if one is communicating with them using stimuli that they recognise as being part of their conversation with themselves, that is, their repertoire, then people with autism always respond. We have to use language that is hard-wired into our partner's brain if we want to capture their attention.

So if 'confirmation' is right at the centre of our understanding of ourselves – and ourselves in relation to other than ourselves – can we deliberately use it to raise the self-esteem and quality of life of people who are struggling so hard in a world that is unpredictable and does not behave in a rational manner? How can we establish the trust between us which we and they so desperately need?

---

207 Damasio AR (1994) *Descartes' Error.* New York: GP Putnam and Sons (p232).
208 Ramachandran VS (2012) *The Tell-Tale Brain.* London: Random House.

At the risk of repeating myself, what is critical is that confirmation must be delivered in such a way as to have meaning for our recipient conversation partner. It needs to contain elements of our partner's 'language', allowing us to tune in to them, particularly putting ourselves alongside their affective state and showing them that we value what they value.

To do this we enter the world that has significance for their brain, building up a conversation that is based upon what they are doing and how they are doing it, not just observing their body language but responding using the same familiar (to them) elements with our own.

I call this reading and acting from their script – which includes not only their movements, sounds and rhythms but also, when it comes to the more able, their activities, themes and interests. When they are verbal, I will work from their images, ideas and prosody (the rhythms of their speech). I don't have a tick list because this would lead me to focus on my list – but listen with every sense focused on my conversation partner. This confirmation gives them confidence to move on, try something new out. It opens the door to progression.

If this sounds complicated, fortunately such give and take in each other's language is not unfamiliar since it is a part of the developmental process that is part of our own make-up. Provided that all was well in our mother-infant relationship, we have all been through this exchange and even if unconsciously, we recognise it. All it requires is that we lay aside our own inhibitions and enjoy being with people on their terms in a way that they also will enjoy.

Now we know the language that has meaning for them we can use it to extend their affective experience of the world around them so that they begin to seek and enjoy being with people.

However, sometimes the intensity of their focus on their inner pathways makes it difficult to see quite how we can ease ourselves into a perseverant pattern where their brain latches onto a single image or idea and the neurons go on firing the same message over and over again, unable to move on, sometimes for hours on end.

In seeking to establish a safe route out of the closed neural circuit (the limited conversation with themselves) that has become habitual, I recall as a child being given a train set, eight curved rails and a shiny green wind-up engine which circled round and round and round the track but, just like thoughts or images that get repeated over and over again in the brain, I soon realised my engine was going nowhere and I stopped playing with it – until someone added a set of points. Now I did not have to take the train off the track but there was the added interest of a choice, staying in the closed loop or moving out. In the same way, if we use a person's body language or interests to engage with them, it's a perfect, or near enough perfect, fit to offer an escape route and to expand horizons.

But one of the questions that has puzzled me about the effectiveness of confirmation is that, at a neurological level, just because the brain spots something that is part of its repertoire, how does this enable it to get out of its perseverant closed circuit? How does the brain escape?

In a discussion on the neural basis of free will, Tse[209] describes how information is encoded and transmitted by 'firing spikes' which cascade through the neural circuits. However, firing rapid bursts of spikes can re-weight the synapses, temporarily altering the degree to which the synapse triggers future spikes and altering the connectivity of an entire circuit, defining new paths that signals can traverse. Tse also uses the railway analogy, 'just as railway switches must be flipped to allow trains to pass, synaptic weights must be reset before brain signals can follow one path through a neural circuit instead of other paths'.

While it is relatively easy to confirm the body language and hence the affective state of another person when it is physically expressed (for example by the sounds or movements or utterances they are making), sometimes we need to look in more depth for precisely what it is that has significance for them. How this is translated may be very specific and is not always the most obvious part of the activity.

Jenny is playing with a doll's house, sorting coloured bricks and plastic animals into separate compartments. She is not in the least interested by our attempts to show interest in her activity. But when she has sorted them to her satisfaction she bounds up in her chair and bounces on it hard. It is only when I do roughly the same, bouncing on mine, that she looks round at me sharply, interested for the first time.

---

209 Tse PU (2013) *The Neural Basis of Free Will* (p28). Cambridge, MA: The MIT Press.

Pippa is 26. She has been moved around from one placement to another and this has led to a deterioration in her responses to the world. When I was asked to see her, she was spending most of her time withdrawn in her room at home, focusing on repetitive behaviours. She can become seriously disturbed when upset, throwing objects at people. In addition to some words, which are now limited, she uses non-verbal sounds to communicate.

When at home Pippa sits crouched up on her sofa repetitively playing with her Etch A Sketch pad and deleting it carefully, first one half and then the other, making a loud ratchet sound. She also plays with and rubs the fingers of her left hand. In a state of sensory confusion, when she focuses on these two behaviours she is in control, she knows what she is doing.

I sit on the bed where she can see me and I make sounds timed to her 'ratcheting'. She begins to listen and to look at me. Her drawing changes from scribble to drawing round her hand. I do the same on my pad and then pretend to erase it but cannot, which she finds funny. I continue to work with her sounds and then offer her my hands which she draws round, first one, then the other and then both together. She then draws round her drinks can. Next she changes her drawing to two triangles arranged so that they include a cross in the form of a diagonal X. She says, 'flag', followed, quite unexpectedly, by 'Union Jack'.

Characteristic of our shared activity are humour and inventiveness, but all within the physical restriction of her Etch A Sketch but also within a framework that has meaning for Pippa, an activity she understands and feels safe to take part in. Within this safe pathway her attention is rewired and her sense of herself is confirmed.

The effects of using confirmation to communicate can be startling and humbling. For example, when I respond to the sound of Oli's breathing rhythm, from being totally closed off, he starts to seek me out. Even when I revisit his class the next day and am talking to his support teachers (having not seen me since we first engaged with each other), he comes and stands behind me and lays his hands very gently on my head for a second or two. It feels like a blessing.

Again, after 20 minutes of working with Pranve's sounds and hand movements, he is no longer afraid of the sound made by the planes: he is more interested in engaging my attention and showing me what he can do. In both situations, attention has been shifted from the inner world to interest in what is going on round them in the world outside, the common factor being my profound interest and involvement in the feedback my partner is giving themselves.

Sometimes more able people are able to make this focal shift for themselves, usually by finding an activity in the world outside that offers a physical reward. For example, Chris says that she is perfectly all right when she is driving. The vibration through the steering wheel and the need to focus on her road skill override her sensory processing problems. An alternative for her is smoking: both are physical sensations on which she can concentrate so that she is excluding excess input. On the other hand, Rod, who is very clever but has been aggressive towards his family, now says he has other things to think about since he has been moved to a school where there is the high level of intellectual demand, which he needs. But neither of these 'normal' occupations put them in touch with people. Jacob Barnet's mother was told he would never read. At the age of 11 he was studying physics at Illinois University and is now, at 14, reading for his Master's Degree in quantum physics and tutoring students. Even here, his mother says she took him out of school and followed his 'passions', in his case the stars, so she started by taking him to a planetarium.

So, on the one hand we are reducing the anxiety related to sensory chaos by using familiar material that does not stress the processing system, and on the other we are shifting attention to some activity that is of overriding significance to the individual.

Flipping the switch

What I am suggesting is that, when the brain is trapped in perseverant messaging and sensory chaos, it is possible that 'confirmation' is an event so powerful (likened to being thrown a life-belt in a stormy sea) that it triggers a cascade of spikes through the neural circuits, re-weighting the synapses. Tse[210] compares this process to reconfiguring the combination on a padlock without opening it. Flipping the switch allows attention and activity to escape to a new direction.

Such redirection does not necessarily need to come in the same mode as our partner's initiative, but nevertheless must be delivered in such a way that it is recognisable as part of their personal language. For example,

---

210 Tse P U (2013) Free Will Unleashed. *New Scientist* **June 2013**.

one might use tapping, or clapping, or touch to echo the rhythm of a sound. Whichever direction these inputs come from, they have to be of a 'lifesaving' quality, sufficient to shift the brain out of its retreat into the body's self-defensive position.

(And if change is an outcome of rapid bursts of spikes, what might failure to reconfigure the synapses say about perseveration?)

Meanwhile, remembering that it is not just what people do but how they do it, in building up our new mutual relationship we learn from each individual their personal life stories as they are reflected in their current psychological state, since these will colour their responses to us. Autistic or not, we are whole people with a life story, not just a present but a present coloured by the past. One way of putting it is that we need to recognise the whole ecosystem of our partner.

The mother-child nature of the need for confirmation of self is brought home to me when I meet Andrew, who has severe autism as well as complex problems. His relationship with his mother (who tries her best to help him), is ambiguous. He constantly breaks his cell phone and demands the latest one. Various strategies have been tried to contain this expensive habit without success. My own intervention is no better in this respect but it does throw some light on why he is so desperate for the latest – and therefore, in his eyes, the 'perfect' – model. In his desperation for connectedness, I realise that it is like a navel cord to him, and I say, 'It's like a piece of string isn't it?' Understanding flashes in his eyes as he does a double-take and agrees with me, giving me full-on attention. 'Yes,' he says. Unable to separate from his mother or to satisfy his need for her, his persistent attempts to recreate this ideal umbilical attachment melt away like mirages.

Anticipatory confirmation

Confirmation in the form of validating what is important is normally used retrospectively, that is, as a response, and is often thought of as 'imitation', 'copying' or 'mimicking'. The problem is that in practice such an approach can lead to a no-through road of games, rituals and the attitude that, 'this is what we do with Jimmy', when what we need to be aiming for is opening out the perseverant loop.

But there is another, often even more effective way of using our partner's language – by getting in first before they start. Anticipatory validation can stop perseveration in its tracks, before it ever takes hold. Having received the confirmation they need to shift their attention, our partner can interact without falling into their inner repetitive loop.

Mitch comes out of the bathroom following his toilet, needing to know he looks good and saying, 'My teeth look white'. If he does not get confirmation he lashes out at someone. So the trick is to say to him, 'Your teeth look white', as soon as the door opens and before he starts to come out and gets locked into his anxious phrase. This simple strategy validates his profound emotional need to be acceptable. He laughs with relief and goes off about his business.

The same strategy is adaptable to almost any situation where our partner is getting locked into the need for physical confirmation – often resulting in aggression or what is seen as challenging behaviour when they do not get it[211]. Perhaps they desire to receive affection in the form of a hug, as we all do at times. Laying aside for the minute mistaken 'no touch' policies, the difficulties they have in processing proprioceptive messages may leave them unable to gauge the strength of their hugs, so that their partner experiences their greeting as embarrassing or painful and tries to withdraw, so they squeeze even tighter. Again, the most effective response is to get in first, holding out your arms as soon as they see you and greeting them with a brief but strong hug before their neediness asserts itself. They do not then have time to fall into the pit of their affective distress.

Vibration

Another approach uses vibration to offer physical confirmation of self. This powerful burst of physical stimulus defines our boundaries and parameters, giving us a physical sense of who we are and helping us to define our sense of self.

Like Chris, when I am driving, I get physical feedback that tells me not only what I am doing but relates me to my environment. I feel the texture of the driving wheel in my hand but also, through vibration, I am being told about the state of the tarmac or concrete surface and the bounce of the potholes – touch and proprioceptive signals instantly co-ordinated with the rolling screen of my visual intake, giving me a physical assessment of my surroundings. Simultaneous, me and it.

---

211 Caldwell P (2012) *Delicious Conversations.* Hove: Pavilion Publishing.

In practice, vibration can be a very important tool. Whereas the internal confirmation our bodies receive from what we see and hear may pass unnoticed, that of vibration presents us with a powerful and more global sense of embodiment. And when a child with autism is not able to engage with an intervention that uses their body language, they may well need this sense of embodiment, of themselves, before they can respond. (I will find it difficult to 'talk' to you if I have no sense of myself.)

The embodying effects of using vibration can be clearly seen in the final section of the training film *Autism and Intensive Interaction*[212], which records an uncut session with Jamie (who we met on p78), showing him tapping himself with a plastic skittle and in his own world, cut off from communication. As we have seen, his response to a vibration unit that I use with him, in the form of a turtle, and my attempts to link this vibration to his sounds, produces dramatic results and draws him quickly into communication with the outside world. When we are finished, he lies back on his teaching assistant's lap and, still holding the vibration unit and turning it on and off, encourages her to rub his leg, taking her hand on and off in synchrony with his turning the unit on and off. He is clearly leading her.

If 'I need you to love me' is the imperative that drives our quest for relationship, 'You matter to me' is the ultimate confirmation. And awakening the possibility of affective engagement is the most important thing we can do for anyone, autistic or not. This is the glue that sticks us together.

Mime

Moving on from immediately contingent interactions, we can use body language to make genuine conversation.

Take a child who sits by a lake all day and throws stones in the water. We could sit beside her and throw a stone when she did, synchronising our actions. But at the same time we need to be asking ourselves what exactly it is she is looking at. Is it the splash or the ripples? Or is it, as I have seen with a man whose fascination with smoking was not apparently to inhale but rather to stand holding his cigarette and watch the smoke as it coiled up into the air, thinned and eventually disappeared, something quite different – an exploration of the boundary between 'here and not here'?

---

212 Caldwell P (2010) *Autism and Intensive Interaction.* Training film. London: Jessica Kingsley Publishers.

In order to explore this possibility we shall need to move from anticipatory confirmation or imitation and immediate response in the form of confirmation, to mime, where we are 'trying to convey (and share) the impression of an idea, emotion or feeling by gesture or movement without using words'[213]. (In our practice we shall have to do this within the boundaries of our partner's language.) Sitting beside the girl throwing stones, for example, we might attempt this by holding our hand (face down) and gently rippling it away, fading the movement and then turning it over and looking with surprise (head back, eyebrows up, mouth open) at the empty palm. With mime, we can share jokes and we can also have retrospective conversations, sharing what is past. In order to do this we tune into the physical circumstances and the psychological effect, the 'how it felt' tone of the original context.

One might object that the person with autism will not grasp such subtlety – but in practice they do recognise expression if it reflects the affective root of their current interest. By careful observation (which involves not just looking at but entering into the feeling of what it is they are fixating on) and using mime to express this, we can bypass verbal blockage and open out interventions that can otherwise so easily get stuck in mimicry. By learning their affective language we are truly sharing what they value, valuing them as they are, rather than trying to frogmarch them into a sensory world that is experienced as totally confusing.

Where access to verbal speech is blocked, as well as using mime to align ourselves with how a person feels, contingent mime can also be used to convey information. A woman who is scared to go out for a walk, which is part of the resource centre's daily programme, hangs on to the door frames and cries, resisting attempts to persuade her to go out. At first I use gesture with speech ('you and I are going for a walk') to convey that we are going out, pointing to her, myself and the door but it makes no difference. So (remembering what Wendy Lawson[214] said about neurotypicals not completing sentences), next time I repeat the gestures but also, point strongly to the floor by her feet and say, 'and then we are coming back again'. Where speech on its own has not made sense to her, through the use of mime (even if accompanied by speech), I have indicated she is returning to somewhere she recognises and where she feels safe. Her distress falls away. She now comes out of the door and goes for a walk.

---

213 The New Oxford English Dictionary of English (1998) Oxford: Clarendon Press.
214 Personal communication with author (undated).

It is worthwhile thinking about and practicing how you might communicate a scenario to a person who is confused by speech (and therefore cannot respond). For example, try taking a strategy (one that has been used successfully): how would you suggest to your partner, without using words, that instead of cramming their mouth with food they take small portions and chew them before swallowing?

Mimicry, imitation and copying draw attention from the inner world to the world outside, drawing the brain towards the source of the 'echo'. But we need to move beyond simply rote learning personal language to using it to facilitate the exploration of each other's worlds. It is like the difference between reading the vocabulary and grammar of a language and speaking with the intention to communicate. One is the product of observation while the other involves total participation.

All the emotions can be expressed through mime; it is the language of affect – a vehicle for total attunement. Rather than one-on-one, it expresses one-*in*-one, bringing us to the heart of intent. Mime can be not just contingent confirmation but affirmation of shared understanding. It can liberate us from (what is for some people with severe autism) the tyranny of words.

Epilogue

The human body is the developmental product of an incredibly delicately poised evolutionary process. On the whole it works: deviations from its basic pathways have consequences, varying all the way from adaptive to disastrous. Not for nothing is the condition we call autism a spectrum.

The attitude adopted by people with autism to the world around them (as expressed by articulate individuals with Asperger's) is coloured not only by their difficulties in interpreting their incoming sensory information but by people's responses to them. It ranges from anger and denial to acceptance and an ability to embrace what the non-spectrum world regards as 'deviation' from normal. Growing up with autism may mean facing the questions, 'why am I different?' and 'what is wrong with me?' And as used by the non-spectrum world, the word 'wrong' gives offence – like the rest of us, our sensory experience tells us that it is we who are right and the rest of the world that is wrong.

Trying to reconcile the internal and external points of view is almost impossible unless we stand outside and examine the pattern emerging from neurological research and the wide differences in formation and development of the nervous system during embryogenesis, probably as the outcome of a number of dissimilar genetic and environmental causes. From a picture of gross damage to the cranial and spinal nerves, to deficits in numbers of nerves transmitting messages from sense organs to the processing systems in the brain, to damage in the cerebellum and an over-active amygdala and sympathetic nervous system, to imbalances in the neurotransmitters at the synapses, the total effect is not only of confusion but also of physiological neuralgia and sometimes psychological pain. Each person with autism is radically different and the ways they deal with the struggle to make sense of what is going on round them also differs.

In this book I have tried to highlight some of these variations, together with their consequences. I do so with deep respect for the individuals I have known and tried to engage with. I have learned much from them about courage and what it is to be human. But I should like to end by returning to William.

William, whose brain works in overdrive, is talking about one of his favourite subjects, the octopus. He asks me if I think that an octopus changes colour not only to disguise itself but also when it feels something? Not a subject I had considered, but an expert tells me that this is possibly true, at least if one considers feeling as sensation rather than affect, since their pigment cells expand altering their colour if they are prodded[215]. (He starts a new train of thought in my mind, for example, does the octopus know that it is feeling? That is, is it both conscious and self-aware?)

But William has finished drawing his anger box and lays down his pen. As we are about to leave, he unexpectedly picks it up and draws a small box in the right hand bottom corner of the page. He comments in a rather off-hand voice:

'That's my good box. I don't talk about it much.'

---

215 Prager EJ (2000) *How do squid and octopuses change color?* [online]. Scientific American. Available at: http://www.scientificamerican.com/article.cfm?id=how-do-squid-and-octopuse (accessed December 2013).

Catch up

The people in this book are alive now and their lives are moving on. Recently, I have been in contact with Christine again and she started to tell me about pain that we had somehow missed in our conversations, pain that is so much a part of her life experience that she did not even mention it before – pain in the jaw relieved by pressure behind the ears. 'I used to go to bed with my head as far back as possible pressed against the bed head with my fingers pushing into the angle of my jaw'. She bangs her head to try and relieve the pain. She has finally seen a psychiatrist who, after a number of tests, has diagnosed her as having trigeminal neuralgia and epilepsy without seizures. The psychiatrist says that, if she is on the spectrum, she has Asperger's syndrome (something I have no doubt about at all). She tells me her jaw has always been misaligned, used to click all the time and once actually got stuck and had to be forcibly repositioned (see Chapter 2). The pain, which is not helped by normal painkillers, is responding to Tegretol. She says that she and her boys (and her autistic friend) find the BOSE headphones helpful. 'It's peaceful like when we are in the mountains', she adds, 'Now I know I'm not mad'.

For those like Amy who have no speech and are unable to say what is happening to them, the wheels of diagnosis grind slowly – but for her, the evidence so far does seem to point towards sensitivity in the cranial nerves. Nearly a year since suspicions were first raised, she has had a scan – but is still awaiting an appointment to see the neurologist.

The last word is with William, who is now eight. He tells me that his good box is not real, it's his brain, and that his brain and his anger box fight with each other. Although he has not yet come round to the idea of an overactive amygdala and sympathetic nervous system, it's only a matter of time. Meanwhile, when we talk about tinted glasses, he laughs and says:

'Maybe I could have some coloured lenses for my imagination?'

Appendix one: An inside out approach

The idea of two worlds, the 'inside world' of autism and the non-spectrum world 'outside', underpins much of Donna Williams' work, particularly her fascinating book *Autism: An inside out approach*[216] (which is almost an encyclopaedia of the world of autism), her poem, *Nobody Nowhere*[217] and the film *Jam-Jar*[218]. Each describe in different ways what she terms, 'The World' and 'My World', the latter being her place of retreat where she can hide from the sensory overload that the world we share imposes on her. Although a place of refuge, 'a place where you just "go", where there is no turmoil, it also is a prison in the sense that all the relationships you should have had with the world outside, you have in there'.

The idea of the inside out approach emphasises the gulf between how our experience of the reality we share leaves those of us who are non-spectrum with a completely different sensory framework from those with autism. The problem being that the non-spectrum world makes behavioural judgements and base strategies on what we perceive, and not what their day-to-day experiences are. Rather than understanding their causes, this is very often the base-line for our social rejection of their so-called bizarre behaviours.

216 Williams D (1988) *Autism: An inside-out approach*. London: Jessica Kingsley.
217 Williams D (1992) *Nobody Nowhere: The remarkable autobiograhy of an autistic girl*. London: Doubleday.
218 Everson S (1995) *Jam-Jar*. UK: Fresh Film. (Film)

Appendix two: Intensive Interaction

I was recently asked to produce five top tips for using Intensive Interaction. Wanting to get a broad view, I made the mistake of canvassing the experience of five top practitioners – and got back around 25 different suggestions. Not easy to put into sets and enough to fill a book, or at least an appendix[219].

But what was interesting was that each clearly reflected their writer's voice, unsurprising perhaps because just like we evolve friendships, Intensive Interaction is about developing a unique relationship with a conversation partner, something we 'share the flavour of', rather than 'do to', each one qualitatively different and totally personal. We all go about it slightly differently. So the summary that is offered (with the help of my co-communicators) is in the sense of guidelines rather than rules. We all develop our own style.

To begin with, Intensive Interaction, or 'Responsive Communication' as I prefer to think of it, uses body language to communicate with partners with whom we find it difficult to get in touch. Usually non-verbal, the approach can also be used to accompany and ease interaction with partners who do have speech, just as we all, autistic or not, use body language (positive and negative) with each other to convey how we feel.

Before we even start, we need to lay aside our own agenda, what we think our partner ought to be doing. This can be difficult in a goal-orientated culture. However, it really does help to empty the mind and place ourselves wholly at the disposal of our partner. Our attitude needs to be, 'I am here for you'. My aim is to be with them and whatever they find interesting in the fullest sense.

---

219 Thanks to Janet Gurney, Penny Mytton, Jemma Swales, Nicola Wightman and Michelle O'Neill.

Personally, although I may spend a little time with staff before getting started (finding out if there is anything my partner particularly dislikes), I do not spend a lot of time in pre-engagement observation (since my mere presence may raise tension) but ease my way in as our encounter presents itself. I avoid verbal introductions, since these set the wrong context. So my initial greeting will reflect a sound they are making, or a movement, or the answer to a rhythm.

Each partner has their own language and I feel like a beginner every time. Sooner or later we are going to have to take the plunge, and the advice here is 'just do it', 'give it a go'. We do not have to be experts – mothers and infants are doing it all the time and it is quite a good idea to borrow a friend's baby to practice on. They are very responsive. But it is crucial to remember that we are not infantilising our partners, treating them as babies. By sending signals that the brain can easily process, we are reducing sensory overload, so that the brain recognises at least something in the environment and can more easily negotiate their everyday experience. Cut out body language and we should present as robots.

Look not only at what they are doing but for the specific physical sensations their action is sending back to the brain. This feedback may not be the same as their action, so try their activity yourself and see what you get out of it. Work from this.

Don't use props. If you do, both your attention and your partner's will focus on what is known as the 'third object'. You may feel naked, but you are the best piece of equipment you have. What is essential to engagement is the one-on-one interaction. The only thing you need is you.

Your partner's language will probably include a number of different elements and the ones that have the most meaning for them and to which they most easily respond are not always the most obvious. Watch out for small movements and rhythms and listen for quiet sounds. These may be very small indeed – as little as breathing rhythm or a scratching finger, anything that your partner is using to give themselves physical feedback. You want to know how it is they are 'talking to themselves'.

Join in, bearing in mind that what you are trying to do is establish conversation, so although you may start by using imitation, think of answering and responding rather than copying or mimicking. Timing is very important – give your partner space to reply (which may mean waiting for some considerable time). Don't rush them: use pauses.

Look not just for what they are doing, but how they are doing it, since this will tell you how they feel. You need to tune in to that feeling with empathy.

Show them you are listening through your own body language. For example, leaving your face open and inclining your head to one side expresses your attention. (And they will be able to decode your body language if you are presenting it in the context of their language.)

Watch the body/face to see if there is any response at all. This may be as little as a flicker of the eyelids, or they may turn to you, give eye contact, show some form of interest. Their expression may become attentive or thoughtful. If they turn away it may be because they wish to withdraw, but alternatively it may be because they are deaf and wish to present their best ear. (If they withdraw, draw back a bit yourself and try again, presenting the sound or movement slightly differently, or try another sound.) Base your next move on their response. Take turns, as in conversation.

Allow your partner to determine proximity. They may feel uncomfortable if you sit too close. I tend to sit beside rather than opposite to avoid direct eye contact, which can be painful. One can even work with sounds from the next room.

Extemporise within the context of their language, using variations drawn from their own repertoire. So movement might be answered by a sound (one of theirs) or a rhythmic movement by tapping. Difference can also be expressed by altering the rhythm slightly. Or put two elements, such as rhythm and sound, together. You will get attention by straight copying but the element of surprise in 'difference' motivates your partner to want to come back for more. 'I recognise that but there is something odd that intrigues my attention.'

Once your partner understands that if they make an initiative they will get an answer, they will normally try testing you out. Look for anything new that your partner introduces, if you miss it you will send the message that you are not listening to them. Within the limits of any learning disability that may or may not be present, they will generalise: 'if I scratch my nose she will respond but what happens if I bang the floor?'

And once we have mastered their language, like a verbal conversation, it does not matter who starts off: we can kick-start interaction by using one of their initiatives. Just say 'Hello' in their language. It might be a wave or tapping that is part of their rhythm or a welcoming sound they recognise as theirs.

Sometimes when there is no response it can feel as though one is being rejected and this can be discouraging. Responses may be small and take time. But the most common difficulty is that we get stuck in a routine or game and start wondering what to do next. This can happen if we just copy – the brain habituates and needs the slight jolt of surprise (given by responding unusually but within their repertoire) to open out the conversation again. (If I was talking to you and repeated the same thing over and over again I should not be surprised if you got bored). Other difficulties are 'over-excitement' and over-attachment. The former can be avoided by remembering the anxiety that is central to the lives of those on the spectrum and avoiding 'hyping them up' by exaggerating their sounds. Always aim to calm and centre your partner by bringing their sounds down. The danger of over-attachment should be addressed by working as a member of a team: involving all those who are engaged with them.

Intensive Interaction is sometimes thought of as being used in sessions but ideally it becomes just part of the way that we interact with our partner, so that, in a confused sensory setting, they are always being offered something that has meaning for them.

Filming or working in pairs really helps us to improve our practice, since we cannot pick up everything that is going on at once and need to go back and reflect on what we are doing and where we have missed out, not in a sense of judgement but so that we can engage more fully with our partners and they with us next time. It is good when they want to be with people.

Interaction is sometimes very powerful and often moving. The final piece of advice from my practitioner colleagues is to relax, enjoy it, and to have fun.

Appendix three: Sensory overload/ the autonomic storm

The following descriptions of what it feels like when sensory overload tips into the sympathetic nervous system, 'blows its fuses', are direct quotations from writers who have experienced them. Akin to panic attacks and tantrums but way up the scale of severity – like catastrophic natural events: an earthquake or tsunami, the individual feels they are being attacked and responds as if this is so.

'A feeling kept washing over me. It was like a tingling in the back of the neck. It began with the feeling one gets from eating lemons. It spread to every fibre of my body like cracks in an earthquake. I knew this monster. It was the Big Black nothingness and it felt like death coming to get me. The walls went up and my ears hurt. I had to get out, out of the room, out of this thing stuck on me, suffocating me in my shell of flesh. A scream rose in my throat. My four-year-old legs ran from one side of the room, moving ever faster and faster, my body hitting the wall like a sparrow flying at the window. My body was shaking. Here it was. Death was here. Don't want to die, don't want to die, don't want to die… the repetition of the words blended into a pattern with only one word standing out, the word die. My knees went to the floor. My hands ran down the mirror. My eyes frantically searched the eyes looking back, looking for meaning, looking for something to connect. No one, nothing, nowhere. Silent screaming rose in my throat. My head seemed to explode. My chest heaved at each final breath at the gates of death. Dizziness and exhaustion began to overtake the terror. It was amazing how many times a day I could be dying and still be alive.'[220]

---

220 Williams D (1992) *Nobody Nowhere: The remarkable autobiograhy of an autistic girl*. London: Doubleday

'All the time I was growing up I experienced a constant shudder down my spine. Periodically the shuddering grew worse, while at other times it kept relatively quiet so I could live with it. It was like that feeling you get before you sneeze, only as if it had got stuck and was suspended in my spine in order to turn into something permanent… I became slightly used to it but it was a constant torture, most noticeably when it changed in intensity. It was like cold steel down my spine. It was hard and fluid at the same time, with metallic fingers drumming and tickling the outside. Like sharp clips digging in to my spine and lemonade inside. Icy heat and digging fiery cold. It was like the sound of screeching chalk on a blackboard turned into a silent concentration of feeling, then placed in the back of my neck. From there, so metallic, the feeling radiated out into my arms, clipped itself into my elbows but never came to an end, never ever came to an end.'[221]

'When they saw the sound of a moped made me act strangely they started scaring me. They would wait for me to pass them and then suddenly rev up. The din made the ground under my feet disappear and I could neither see nor feel the world round me. Up and down were suddenly in the same place and I had no idea where my feet were. So as not to fall over or explode from inside, I had to grab the fence where I was standing, pressing myself against it and holding on hard. I had to feel something that stood still, something anchored in a world that had become totally unpredictable.'[222]

'I would do anything to stop it, bang my head against a wall, run in front of a car.[223]

'It's almost impossible for me to keep my emotions contained. Once I've made a mistake, the fact of it starts rushing towards me like a tsunami. And then, like trees and houses being destroyed by the tsunami, I get destroyed by the shock. I get swallowed up in the moment and can't tell the right response from the wrong response. All I know is I have to get out of the situation as soon as I can so I don't drown. To get away I'll do anything. Crying, screaming and throwing things, hitting out even…'[224]

---

221 Gerland G (1996) *A Real Person*. London: Souvenir Press.
222 *Ibid.*
223 Weeks L (undated) *A Bridge of Voices*. Documentary audiotape, BBC Radio 4. Produced by Tom Morton for Sandprint Programs.
224 Higashida N (2013) *The Reason I Jump: The inner voice of a thirteen-year-old-boy with autism*. London: Sceptre.

In a series of written communications, Carly[225] talks about the pain that underlay her flailing:

'I feel the pain course through my body and it's unbearable.'

Hitting her head helps her to cope. She says people should 'back off and let me be. Most of the time I am having a power struggle with myself.'

'My body… does not always do what I want it to do. It feels like my insides are being ripped out of my body… the pain is unbearable.'

Donna Williams talks about self-injury:

'There was a rip through the centre of my soul. Self-abuse was the outward sign of an earthquake nobody saw. I was like an appliance during a power surge. As I blew fuses my hands pulled out my hair and slapped my face. My teeth bit my flesh like an animal bites the bars of its cage, not realising the cage was my own body. My legs ran round in manic circles, as though they could outrun the body they were attached to. My head hit whatever was next to it, like someone trying to crack open a nut that had grown too large for its shell. There was an overwhelming feeling of inner deafness – deafness to self that would consume all that was left in a fever pitch of silent screaming.'[226]

225 Fleischmann A & Fleischmann C (2012) *Carly's Voice: Breaking through autism* (p302). New York: Touchstone.
226 Williams D (1992) *Somebody Somewhere*. London: Doubleday.

PLEASE NOTE:

The contact details for the Irlen Lens Centre on p145 have changed to:

7a Stowupland Road
Stowmarket
Suffolk
IP14 5AG

tel: 07745333314
email: info@irleneast.com
web: www.irleneast.com

Sensory problems: useful equipment

Vision

Irlen lenses
Coloured light bulbs
Dimmer switches
Peaked caps
Grey sunglasses (where the problem is caused by intensity of light rather than colour or pattern)
Contacts for Colorometric test

Irlen Lens Centre, 4 Park Farm Business Centre, Fornham St. Genevieve, Bury St. Edmunds, Suffolk, IP28 6TS 01284 724301
Contact local Dyslexia Society for information regarding local practitioners.

Sound

BOSE Quiet Comfort 15 Acoustic Noise Reduction Headphones (cuts down on distant sound while allowing close up conversation).
Alternatively, contact a good music technician who should be able to measure the frequencies that are causing pain and using a specially designed acoustic material, build this into headphones that cut these out.

Balance, boundary and nerve pain problems

Inputs need to be frequent, topping up with short sessions several times a day to make any real difference.

Trampoline

Pogo stick

Swing

Space hopper

Climbing frame, wall or bars

Exercise sandals with ridges inside

Astroturf to walk on

Weights

Weighted clothes, carrying rucksack or shopping bags with books or drink cans in them

Weighted blankets

Compression vests/stockings

Sheet of lycra – good way of applying pressure to head as well as body (use under supervision)

Athletes pressure vest

Biohug vest (Google 'Biohug' for details)

Vibration and firm massage